INTRODUCTION

to

REHABILITATION

READINESS

Marianne Farkas
Anne Sullivan Soydan
Cheryl Gagne

CENTER *for* PSYCHIATRIC REHABILITATION
Sargent College of Health and Rehabilitation Sciences

BOSTON
UNIVERSITY

Center for Psychiatric Rehabilitation
Boston University
940 Commonwealth Avenue West
Boston, MA 02215

http://www.bu.edu/cpr/

THE CENTER FOR PSYCHIATRIC REHABILITATION was established in 1979 in response to the recognition of the need for additional knowledge and skills to help to improve the lives of persons with severe psychiatric disabilities. The center is affiliated with Boston University's Sargent College of Health and Rehabilitation Sciences and is staffed by professionals from many disciplines who have national reputations in the fields of rehabilitation and mental health.

The mission of the center is the development, demonstration, dissemination, and utilization of the new knowledge and technology contributing to the recovery of people with severe mental illness.

The Center for Psychiatric Rehabilitation is supported in part by the National Institute on Disability and Rehabilitation Research and the Center for Mental Health Services, Substance Abuse and Mental Health Services Administration.

CONTENTS

LIST OF TABLES

ACKNOWLEDGMENTS

We wish to acknowledge first and foremost consumer survivors of psychiatric disability who have been willing to form partnerships with us, generously giving us their time and the learning they derived from their own recovery and rehabilitation journey.

We wish to acknowledge Bill Anthony, Executive Director of the Center for Psychiatric Rehabilitation at Boston University, who has provided his leadership and vision for the past 25 years. We wish to acknowledge the rest of our colleagues at the Center for Psychiatric Rehabilitation whose ongoing work in recovery and rehabilitation has provided us with valuable input for this text.

We wish to acknowledge Art Dell Orto, Chair of the Rehabilitation Counseling Department, Sue McNamara, and Pat Nemec who supported, piloted, and helped to develop the technology for Rehabilitation Readiness.

We wish to acknowledge our colleagues at the BCPR Consulting, Inc., who, under the leadership of Bill Kennard and Rick Forbess, have provided us invaluable feedback from the field of mental health and rehabilitation.

We would like to especially acknowledge Linda Getgen whose creativity and long suffering patience brought this book to production.

MF
AS
CG

Dedicated to

Mikal R. Cohen, PhD, September 5, 1946–March 2, 1999
and
Karen Sue Danley, PhD, July 5, 1941–April 23, 1998

Colleagues, friends, innovators, pioneers in the field, and
unceasing advocates for individuals with psychiatric disabilities.

CHAPTER 1 *The Context for Rehabilitation Readiness*

INTRODUCTION

Determining which clients are committed to change and then promoting clients' willingness to engage in a change process is arguably one of the most difficult tasks facing clinicians. Investigators such as Prochaska (1991) and Tsang, Lam, Ng, and Leung (2000) have attempted to use variables such as socioeconomic status, age, gender, and problem characteristics, (e.g., duration, intensity, and type of symptoms) to predict those who will not commit to such a process or who will drop out from therapy. These variables have not proven useful in determining who is ready for therapy and who is not.

In the psychiatric rehabilitation field, the issue of rehabilitation readiness emerges frequently because active client involvement in the rehabilitation is central to the process. Psychiatric rehabilitation is designed to help people with a serious psychiatric disability choose, get, and keep a particular role in the setting that they prefer (Anthony, Cohen & Farkas, 1990). The client-practitioner partnership that is involved in supporting a person's determination of his or her own goal seems to imply that rehabilitation is only appropriate for those clients who function at the highest levels (Anthony, Cohen & Farkas, 1987; Anthony et al., 1990). In other words, many clinicians feel that only high functioning clients are ready to participate in rehabilitation. This perception persists despite solid evidence that psychiatric rehabilitation has been successfully used with individuals with even the most severe psychiatric disabilities (e.g., Shern, Tsemberis, Anthony et al., 2000; Shern, Tsemberis, Winarski et al., 1997). Mental

> The process of rehabilitation readiness is designed to help consumers feel more confident, aware, and committed to their rehabilitation.

health and rehabilitation practitioners routinely restrict opportunities to participate in normal work, educational, residential, and social environments based on the mistaken belief that rehabilitation is not appropriate for their particular client or that their clients are not ready to make use of rehabilitation activities (Cohen, Anthony & Farkas, 1997). Surveys of consumer preferences indicate, however, that most people with psychiatric disabilities do want to participate and feel included in natural community settings (Tanzman, 1993; Rogers, Danley, Anthony, Martin & Walsh, 1994). The process of Rehabilitation Readiness is designed to help consumers feel more confident, aware, and committed to their rehabilitation (Cohen et al., 1997).

Introduction to Rehabilitation Readiness discusses the process of helping an individual assess and develop his or her preparedness for the work involved in psychiatric rehabilitation. It also clarifies common terms used in the field and briefly describes the current state of the field of mental health and rehabilitation. Additionally, it outlines the process of psychiatric rehabilitation (Anthony, Cohen, Farkas & Gagne, 2001) and the concepts involved in the technology for assessing and developing readiness (Farkas, Cohen, McNamara, Nemec & Cohen, 2000; Cohen, Forbess & Farkas, 2000; Cohen, Nemec & Farkas, 2000).

Clarification of Terms

The field of mental health and psychiatric rehabilitation uses a plethora of terms to refer to the nature of the difficulty or problem being addressed by psychiatric rehabilitation, the individual with the difficulty, and the person working with that individual. The variety of terms used creates not only confusion but also polarizes the constituents of psychiatric rehabilitation because the terms often represent a particular philosophical point of view or opinion. For example, some people feel that people with schizophrenia are people who have a "mental illness." Others believe that it is more useful to refer to people as having a "psychiatric experience." Those who believe in using the term *mental illness* feel it is disingenuous and even harmful not to be direct and use the term. Those who believe in using the term *psychiatric experience* do not feel that the problems are, in fact, an illness and feel it is short sighted and stigmatizing to not to use the term. The following section clarifies the terms used in this text.

The Nature of the Difficulty Addressed by Psychiatric Rehabilitation

The first terms to be clarified are those that describe the type of difficulties for which psychiatric rehabilitation was designed. Various terms have been used both in mental health/rehabilitation literature and in practice: *psychiatric illness, impairment, psychiatric disability, emotional problems, psychiatric background,* and *psychiatric experience.* The variety of terms indicates varying points of view about the nature of the problem and the extent to which "mental illness" is an illness or a sociopolitical problem (Chamberlin, 1990). This text uses *psychiatric disability,* in preference to other terms when referring to the aspect of the problem which psychiatric rehabilitation addresses. The term *psychiatric disability* does not speak to the issue of the cause of mental illness nor does it imply that a particular psychiatric diagnosis is either correct or useful. In using the term *disability,* rather than *illness,* reference is made to the restriction in functioning experienced by some people with a psychiatric diagnosis of major mental illness or a long term psychiatric experience. The term *impairment* is used to refer to what is typically thought of as psychiatric symptoms or the personal distress related to the psychiatric difficulty or problem.

The Individual with the Psychiatric Disability

The individual with psychiatric "experience" or psychiatric disability is referred to in this text variously as: *consumer, consumer-survivor, client,* or *person.* The terms used reflect both the evolution of the field and the current debate within it. The debate centers on the question of what mode of identification most accurately portrays the individual's actual situation or enhances the individual's potential integration as a valued member of society (Caras, 1994; Fisher, 1994). *Consumer* or *consumer survivor* is a generic term used to refer to the relationship of the individual to the mental health system. The terminology of *con-*

sumer (i.e. one who "consumes" or actively uses services and/or a *survivor,* (i.e., one who has "survived" psychiatric or mental health treatment) invokes the personal experience of the individual. Many, but not all consumer organizations, use these terms. The term *client* is used to refer to someone's role in a specific helping relationship with a practitioner or helper. The term *person, people,* or *individual* is used most frequently in this text as an abbreviated form of the phrase: *person with a psychiatric disability.* It is used to underscore the fact that rehabilitation is interested in the human being across all of his or her roles (e.g., client, consumer, tenant, worker, parent, friend, student).

The Individual Providing Rehabilitation

Blankertz, Robinson, Baron, Hughes, and Rutman (1995) surveyed the psychosocial rehabilitation workforce. The survey showed that 40% of these workers were people who had trained in the "core disciplines" (e.g., psychology, social work, nursing, and psychiatry). The rest had a variety of backgrounds, including rehabilitation counselors, mental health counselors, and paraprofessionals. Increasingly, mental health consumers are being hired as providers of mental health services (Moxley & Mowbray, 1997). Consumer-oriented and consumer-provided services are seen as a fundamental aspect of a progressive mental health system (Anthony, 1994). The inclusion of consumers into the mental health and rehabilitation workforce has been occurring over the past 10 years at every level of service provision—direct service, administrative, and supervisory roles (Zipple, Drouin, Armstrong, Brooks, Flynn & Buckley, 1997).

Given the variety of backgrounds of people providing psychiatric rehabilitation services, generic terms best describe the broadest range of the formal and informal workforce. Most frequently the individual providing rehabilitation services is referred to as *practitioner* or *service provider.* Similar to the term *client,* the term *practitioner* describes a role. Some practitioners are consumer professionals and some are not. This text does not use different terms to refer to practitioners who have consumer experience from those who do not. At times, the term *helper* is used. *Helper* is a more generic term that refers to the fact that not all rehabilitation is provided in formal agency settings. Some self-help groups have adapted the technology of psychiatric rehabilitation for use in a self-help organization. Some family members have been trained to use the technology with their family member who has a psychiatric disability. The intermittent use of the term *helpers* in this text serves to remind the reader that many different types of individuals have and will use the process of Rehabilitation Readiness.

CURRENT STATE OF THE FIELDS OF MENTAL HEALTH AND REHABILITATION

It has been estimated that in the United States, 2.6% of the population have a serious psychiatric disorder (SAMSHA, 1993). Several definitions of severe psychiatric disability characterize this target population (NIMH, 1987; SAMHSA, 1993; Goldman, Gattozzi & Taube, 1981). Not only do these definitions share common elements, (such as a diagnosis of mental illness of prolonged duration with resulting major functional incapacity) it is now also possible to operationalize these common elements (IAPSRS, 1997; Ruggeri, Leese,Thronicroft, & Tansella, 2000). "Prolonged duration" has been operationalized as having a "major mental illness for a duration of two or more years" (NIMH, 1987). The U.S. Department of Substance Abuse and Mental Health Services Administration (SAMHSA) has defined major functional impairment as including one of the following:

- Either planned or attempted suicide at some time during the past 12 months,

- *or* lacked a legitimate productive role,

- *or* had a serious role impairment in their main productive roles,

- *or* had serious interpersonal impairment as a result of being totally socially isolated, lacking intimacy in social relationships, showing inability to confide in others, and lacking social support (IAPSRS, 1997).

Within this population are subpopulations, such as young adults (e.g., Harris & Bergman, 1987; Pepper & Ryglewicz, 1984), persons from minority cultures (e.g., Musser-Granski & Carrillo, 1997), persons who are homeless (e.g., Salit, Kuhn, Hartz, Vu & Mosso 1998), or persons otherwise impoverished (e.g., Ware & Goldfinger, 1997), senior citizens (e.g., Gaitz, 1984), persons with both a severe physical disability and severe psychiatric disability (e.g., Pelletier, Rogers & Thurer, 1985), persons who are also developmentally disabled (e.g., Reiss, 1987), persons with substance abuse problems (e.g., Struening & Padgett, 1990).

The concept of disability associated with this varied target group has been dramatically changing due, in part, to the influence of the field of rehabilitation. The old assumption that disability precluded growth and development and prevented people with severe psychiatric disability from full citizenship in their communities is finally fading (Moxley, 1994; Farkas, Gagne & Anthony, 1997). Practitioners and policy makers alike have begun to understand that serious impairment does not necessarily mean life long disability. Anthony (1993) suggests that the term *chronicity* may now be an anachronism, and several authors believe that there is reason for increased hopefulness in the prognosis for people suffering from serious impairment (Ciompi, 1980; Harding, Brooks, Ashikaga, Strauss & Breier, 1987a; Harding, Zubin & Strauss, 1992; Tsuang & Winokur, 1975). Hopefulness about the prognosis of the course of impairment has become a focus for mental health and rehabilitation services in the emergence of the vision of "recovery" (Anthony, 1993).

What Is Recovery?

Recovery has best been described in the writing of consumer-survivors (Houghton, 1982; Deegan, 1988; Granger, 1994; McDermott, 1990). Recovery is described as a deeply personal, unique process of changing one's attitudes, values, feelings, goals, skills, and/or roles. It is a way of living a satisfying, hopeful, and contributive life even with limitations caused by the impairment. Recovery involves the development of new meaning and purpose in one's life as one grows beyond the catastrophic effects of an impairment (Anthony, 1993).

The recovery process has been described as a process that may occur in stages (Spaniol, Koehler & Hutchinson, 1994; Strauss, Hafez, Lieberman & Harding, 1985; Davidson & Strauss, 1992; Young & Ensing, 1999). Recovery is not a linear process. It may be characterized as a struggle that is marked by periods of loss and gain, activity and stasis, or rest. People on the road to recovery experience phases in their recovery that resemble some of the stages of adjustment to loss and grief: denial, anger, resignation, and acceptance. While insufficient research has been done to determine exactly what contributes to recovery, recovery has value as an overall vision for mental health services (Anthony, 1993). The vision of recovery can propel the field forward, much as the vision of ending smallpox in the world or finding a cure for cancer provided inspiration and direction for medical research and treatment.

> Recovery involves the development of new meaning and purpose in one's life as one grows beyond the catastrophic effects of an impairment.

The past decade has witnessed several trends that have laid the foundation for the emergence of the concept of recovery. The first has been the shift from "one stop" treatment delivered within a long stay hospital to multiple services provided by multiple organizations. This shift resulted in the recognition that community based service delivery and service systems had to respond to a comprehensive array of needs and wants rather than simply those related to the pathology itself (Anthony, Kennard, O'Brien & Forbess, 1986). The second trend evolved from a series of long term follow-up studies in the United States and Europe, and Japan (Harding, Brooks, Ashikaga, Strauss & Brier 1987b; Ciompi, 1980; Tsuang, Woolson, & Fleming, 1979; Ogawa, Miya, Watari, Nakazawa, Yuasa & Utena, 1987) that had remarkably similar results. These studies, reviewed by Harding and Zahniser (1994), found that one-half to two-thirds of the cohorts studied improved significantly, as measured by: reduction or elimination of symptoms; decreased use of medication; and the extent to which the individuals were considered "reintegrated" by their family and friends. The findings directly challenged the notion that people with serious psychiatric disabilities had no future other than deterioration or, at best, maintenance. Consequently, new research is investigating the components of success, (e.g.,

Russinova, Ellison & Foster, 1999), rather than focusing predominantly on relapse and failure as the expected outcome. Lastly, the field is slowly recognizing the contribution of consumer-survivors themselves to the development and provision of services. As more consumer-survivors are taking their place as employees in the mental health system, it is more difficult to maintain the myth that recovery is not a possible vision for the system as a whole (Curtis, 1993; Moxley & Mowbray, 1997; Solomon, Draine, & Delaney, 1995). Progressive mental health systems now use the overall mission of facilitating recovery to organize and integrate the efforts of their services.

The concepts of recovery and rehabilitation both involve an orientation toward the present and future rather than focus on the past. They both imply goals related to growth and hopefulness rather than goals reflecting maintenance at current levels. Rehabilitation and recovery are related, yet these concepts differ. The concept of rehabilitation will be discussed and clarified in the following section.

What Is Psychiatric Rehabilitation?

Psychiatric rehabilitation is a field, an approach, and a service for people with serious psychiatric difficulties. It is neither one technique nor a specific program model but rather a practice that may use many techniques and different program models. Psychiatric rehabilitation is a specialized field of study within the field of rehabilitation. As a field, psychiatric rehabilitation encompasses a philosophy and a body of knowledge used in a variety of settings to promote people with psychiatric disability's quest for reintegration into society. The field of psychiatric rehabilitation focuses on the vocational domain but works with individuals to achieve goals in residential and educational domains as well.

The *psychiatric rehabilitation approach* (Anthony et al., 2001) is a particular approach within the field of psychiatric rehabilitation. The approach is based on the traditions of the field of rehabilitation per se, as well as those of psychology. It includes a philosophy, values, a set of principles, and a helping process. The approach can be used within a rehabilitation service and can be implemented in many different program models.

The psychiatric rehabilitation approach derives its basic principles from the tradition of rehabilitation (Anthony et al., 1990). One example of such a principle is the notion that the person's needs, strengths, and deficits can only be viewed within the context of a specific environment. In other words, a person is only skilled or unskilled in relation to the demands of a particular place and role that the person desires. A person who wants to be a part-time bank teller will have different skill requirements than a person who wants to be a part-time student in a home study high school equivalency program. "Selecting appropriate clothing" may be an essential skill for a bank teller's success, but may not matter at all for a part-time student studying at home. Skill assessments, plans, and interventions have to be focused on the extent to which the individual can perform exactly what is needed to be successful and personally satisfied in the particular role and setting the person has chosen. Regardless of whether the disability is physical, intellectual, or emotional, neither instruments such as assessments of global functioning nor standardized skill teaching programs, therefore, can provide the specific results required by a rehabilitation service.

In addition to having roots in the field of rehabilitation per se, the approach also draws from the traditions of psychotherapy and psychology. The philosophy and techniques of client centered psychotherapy (Rogers, 1961; Carkhuff & Berenson, 1977; Carkhuff, 1981) and the understanding and interventions derived from cognitive, educational, developmental, and behavioral psychology all contributed to the rehabilitation approach (Farkas, Anthony & Cohen, 1989). Each of these contributes to the overall understanding of the person and the psychiatric rehabilitation approach. Client centered psychotherapy contributes both the philosophy and techniques needed to establish a respectful partnership with the client (Rogers, 1957). A respectful, empowering relationship is the cornerstone of the entire rehabilitation process. Techniques such as demonstrating understanding (sometimes also called "empathic listening" or "active listening"), inspiring, and self-disclosure promotes the strong connection that is the basis for partnership between the client and the practitioner.

Cognitive rehabilitation techniques contribute strategies for increasing the clients understanding and ability to concentrate on the process components by orienting clients to each rehabilitation activity. In addition cognitive therapy contributes to rehabilitation strategies used in overcoming barriers to learning a new skill (Stuve, Erickson & Spaulding, 1991; Brenner, Hodel, Roder & Corrigan, 1992; Corrigan & Storzbach, 1993; Kern & Green, 1998). These include such techniques such as repetition, presenting information in both small concrete segments and integrated practice so that even those people with severe cognitive and concentration limitations can fully participate in a partnership during the complex process of goal attainment.

Educational psychology contributes techniques related to skill teaching and coaching (Carkhuff & Berenson, 1977). Techniques for developing skill-based curriculum, engaging people in a learning process, providing positive and negative feedback in a facilitative manner, analyzing learning difficulties, and the development of practice opportunities stem from educational psychology. Developmental psychology contributes to the understanding of concepts such as "vocational maturity" (Crites, 1961). Vocational maturity describes a continuum of readiness for work based upon a person's previous experience and developmental stage. Danley (1997) further elaborates these stages and their implications for vocational psychiatric rehabilitation. She defines the types of questions related to career development and work that are important to explore with a client before developing a vocational goal.

Behavioral psychology contributes techniques related to the development of skill use, such as the use of rehearsal, rewards, and cueing techniques (Bellack & Mueser, 1990). Such techniques increase the likelihood that clients will use their skill competencies in the appropriate environment at the appropriate time. The psychiatric rehabilitation approach is a systematic synthesis of the learning derived from these fields, based on a specific set of values. Table 1 (Key Rehabilitation Values) presents a list of eight values that forms the basis for a psychiatric rehabilitation philosophy.

> **Psychiatric rehabilitation is a field, an approach, and a service for people with serious psychiatric difficulties.**

Table 1— Key Rehabilitation Values

Person orientation: A focus on the human being as a whole, rather than as a diagnostic label or illness.

Functioning: A focus on performance of everyday activities.

Support: A focus on providing assistance for as long as it is needed and wanted.

Environmental specificity: A focus on the specific context of where a person lives, learns, or works.

Involvement: A focus on including individuals as full partners in all aspects of rehabilitation.

Choice: A focus on the person's preferences throughout the process.

Outcome orientation: A focus on evaluating rehabilitation in terms of the impact on client outcomes.

Growth potential: A focus on improvement in a person's success and personal satisfaction, regardless of the person's current difficulties.

Adapted from Farkas, M. D., Anthony, W. A., & Cohen, M. R. (1989). Psychiatric rehabilitation: the approach and its programs. In M. D. Farkas & W. A. Anthony (Eds.), *Psychiatric rehabilitation programs: Putting theory in to practice* (p. 8). Baltimore: Johns Hopkins University Press.

Key Values of Psychiatric Rehabilitation

Person Orientation. The first key value guiding psychiatric rehabilitation is that of person orientation. Rehabilitation is a process that involves people as individuals. Rehabilitation builds a relationship with the whole person, his or her interests, values, talents, hopes, and fears, rather than relating to the patient role, diagnostic label, or the illness. An individual may expresses fear, for example, about presenting himself at his school application interview after having dropped out of school 10 years before. A rehabilitation practitioner will help the person to first view his fear as the common response of anyone in the same situation, rather than automatically viewing this response as a symptom of his pathology. Another client may be unclear or impulsive about her career path. The rehabilitation practitioner, adhering to the value of person orientation, will work with the person to identify the types of exploration activities needed to clarify her decision, rather than viewing the lack of clarity as symptomatic of poor judgment. Being

> Being oriented to the person...means that the interaction between the practitioner and the client is that of two human beings in a respectful relationship.

oriented to the person also means that the interaction between the practitioner and the client is that of two human beings in a respectful relationship. The practitioner may disclose his or her own personal experiences or preferences to build the relationship or to clarify some aspect of the person's rehabilitation struggle. The client may, at some point, become the practitioner's teacher, providing some information or skill to help the practitioner out, rather than simply keeping the relationship within the traditional boundaries of practitioner and client. The helping relationship prioritizes the person who wants help. The relationship is, obviously, not the place for the practitioner to get help for his or her own emotional problems, however, it does allows two people to meet and develop some level of personal closeness.

Functioning. Second, rehabilitation is designed to improve functioning. The focus of rehabilitation is on improving functioning rather than on reducing symptoms or increasing insights. Functioning can include a person's specific strengths as well as a person's specific deficits. Psychiatric rehabilitation therefore focuses on interventions that develop positive behaviors as opposed to interventions that control negative behavior. Functioning has to do with the performance of everyday activities (e.g., negotiating conflict, analyzing money available, preparing meals) and is, therefore, not mysterious or esoteric. The focus on everyday activities is understandable to most people. The value placed on functioning also implies that psychiatric rehabilitation is not focused on achieving the same level for everyone, but looks for personally relevant improvement.

Support. The third value is the provision of support. Most practitioners, regardless of their orientation, view themselves as offering assistance to their clients. In psychiatric rehabilitation, the assistance is given for as long as it is needed and wanted. The degree of support offered is a function of how much support a person wants to have. Most people have a preference as to the intensity and the length of time during which they experience assistance as supportive. When assistance is offered, either from a practitioner or anyone else, that is either not wanted, or given in a way that is not wanted or at a time that is not wanted, it is not experienced as support. It is experienced as interference.

Environmental specificity. The fourth value is environmental specificity. People with or without disabilities tend to function differently in different environments. For example, a person may be able to negotiate differences at work but be unable to negotiate differences with relatives at home. Psychiatric rehabilitation focuses on assessing persons in relationship to the demands of the particular environments they have chosen. Psychiatric rehabilitation is concerned with helping people to then improve their functioning in a particular living, learning, working, and/or social environment. The environments that are of importance to psychiatric rehabilitation are settings in which there are valued roles in society. Valued roles include roles such as tenant, student, colleague, or club member. In other words, naturally occurring environments or "real world" environments in the living, learning, working, and/or social domains are the focus of rehabilitation efforts.

> The degree of support offered is a function of how much support a person wants to have.

Involvement. The fifth value is involvement. People have the right to be involved in all aspects of work that affects them and others with similar concerns. Most critical to client involvement are the practitioner's commitment to the goal of client involvement and the practitioner's belief that rehabilitation is done with clients and not to clients. Client involvement requires rehabilitation procedures that can be explained to and understood by the client. The rehabilitation intervention cannot seem mysterious to the client. The practitioner must constantly try to demystify rehabilitation. People do not get rehabilitated. They must be "active and courageous participants in their own rehabilitation" (Deegan, 1988, p. 12). Involvement is also expressed in the way in which a rehabilitation program or service is delivered. Efforts are made to involve consumers in the development of the program itself (e.g., the program activities; the rules and policies). At a system level, efforts are made to involve consumers in decision making that affects the delivery of rehabilitation programs. Because of this key value, rehabilitation practitioners can easily join with consumers to advocate for consumer influence throughout the system in any area that affects people with psychiatric disabilities.

> **Most critical to client involvement are the practitioner's commitment to the goal of client involvement and the practitioner's belief that rehabilitation is done with clients and not to clients.**

Choice. The sixth value is choice. While it may seem obvious to state that people with psychiatric disabilities are in fact citizens of the country in which they live, many people with psychiatric disabilities are not accorded the full rights of citizenship. Usually, citizenship means having the right to choose where to live, where to work, and whether or where to go to school. Many people with psychiatric disabilities are not given this opportunity. Furthermore, citizenship in most countries implies that the person has the right to choose whether or not the person wishes to receive assistance. Many people with psychiatric disabilities have no choice about receiving or not receiving an intervention. People with psychiatric disabilities will not be full citizens until these same rights are accorded them. The psychiatric

> **Whether the choice is explicit or implicit, clients, like all people, are more apt to strive to succeed where they have chosen to be.**

rehabilitation approach provides the person with the skills and supports necessary to achieve whatever level of choice the person wishes to make. The clients in a psychiatric rehabilitation program, for example, are seen as having the right to choose rather than be placed in an environment. Aside from the inherent decency of valuing self-determination, it is practical to have people with psychiatric disabilities openly choose where they live, learn, socialize, and/or work. Whether the choice is explicit or implicit, clients, like all people, are more apt to strive to succeed where they have chosen to be.

Outcome orientation. The seventh value reflected in psychiatric rehabilitation is an outcome orientation. Psychiatric rehabilitation is oriented toward an observable outcome rather than simply toward the provision of service. Its goal is not to provide clients with counseling and support services but rather to help clients achieve increased functioning and satisfaction in an environment of their choice. In program evaluation, this means that a psychiatric rehabilitation program does not measure merely the provision of services (e.g., the number of hours of services that are provided). Rather, outcomes in psychiatric rehabilitation are defined as the level of success and satisfaction of clients in the environments of their choice. Success is measured in terms of the person's ability to respond to the demands of the chosen environment; while satisfaction is measured in terms of the person's own reported experience there.

> **Outcomes in psychiatric rehabilitation are defined as the level of success and satisfaction of clients in the environments of their choice.**

Growth potential. The last value reflected in rehabilitation is belief in people's potential for growth. As stated in the discussion of the first value, the aim of psychiatric rehabilitation is more than maintaining people at their current level of functioning. The focus is on success and personal satisfaction in a chosen environment, regardless of the person's current level of functioning. Everyone is considered to have the potential to grow. In some instances, the immediate focus may need to be on maintaining the improvement if there is a danger of the functioning deteriorating. As Strauss (1986) suggested, the process of recovery may

> **Everyone is considered to have the potential to grow.**

require some time spent at one plateau of functioning before moving on to another stage of improvement. Helping people stabilize themselves is important. While maintenance may be an immediate objective, it is never the overall purpose of psychiatric rehabilitation.

The Psychiatric Rehabilitation Process

The philosophy and values of the psychiatric rehabilitation approach, described more fully in Anthony et al. (2001), are put into practice using the psychiatric rehabilitation process. The psychiatric rehabilitation process is a sequenced set of activities that engages people as active partners in choosing their own vision of what a meaningful role and setting would be. The process then organizes the skill and support interventions to make that choice a reality (Table 2—The Three Phases of the Psychiatric Rehabilitation Process). Individual are either taught the skills that they do not currently know, how to overcome the barriers to using the skill they already possess, how to link with existing supports and resources, or how to create new resources where none exist. The skills required to perform these activities are the skills taught in the *Psychiatric Rehabilitation Technology Technology* series (Cohen, Danley & Nemec, 1985; Cohen, Farkas & Cohen, 1986; Cohen, Nemec, Farkas & Forbess, 1988; Cohen, Farkas, Cohen & Unger, 1991; Farkas et al., 2000; Cohen, Forbess & Farkas, 2000; Cohen, Nemec & Farkas, 2000). One component of the training series is Rehabilitation Readiness, as described in *Assessing Readiness for Rehabilitation* (Farkas et al., 2000) and *Developing Readiness for Rehabilitation* (Cohen, Forbess & Farkas, 2000).

Any helper or practitioner who has been trained in the philosophy, values, and techniques of the process can practice psychiatric rehabilitation (Rogers, Cohen, Danley, Hutchinson & Anthony, 1986). Professional discipline and personal experience may contribute to a practitioner's ability to deliver psychiatric rehabilitation, but the only prerequisite is the ability to demonstrate specific skills of the process with a client. The ability to perform psychiatric rehabilitation skills is best reviewed by an expert in the techniques of the process. Psychiatric rehabilitation training is the most common method of acquiring these competencies.

Psychiatric rehabilitation is an approach used within a rehabilitation service. A mental health or rehabilitation service is a component of an organization or system of helping that is focused on decreasing impairment, overcoming disability, or lessening the impact of disadvantage. Impairment, disability, and disadvantage are designations developed by the World Health Organization (Wood, 1980) to describe aspects of the impact of severe psychiatric difficulties. Examples of services within a comprehensive array of services, unified by a vision of recovery, are represented in Table 3. Each service is distinguished by its impact. For example, impairment (the basic disorder in thought or feeling) can be impacted by treatment services reducing symptoms or alleviating distress; crisis intervention services improving the clients' safety; case management services that provide clients access to treatment or crisis intervention, as well as wellness services that promote physical health and thereby reduce or limit the effects of the impairment. Rehabilitation is one critical service in a comprehensive mental health system. The outcome of a rehabilitation service is improved role functioning for its clients. Rehabilitation impacts on disability (restricted functioning) and disadvantage (limited opportunities) by either improving the client's skills and supports, or modifying the environment.

> **Rehabilitation impacts on disability (restricted functioning) and disadvantage (limited opportunities) by either improving the client's skills and supports, or modifying the environment.**

In further clarifying psychiatric rehabilitation, it is helpful to correct some common misconceptions about the approach. Psychiatric rehabilitation is not a specific program model. That is, it is not "day treatment for people with serious mental impairments" nor "a hospital program for people with serious impairment" nor a specific kind of vocational program. The psychiatric rehabilitation approach can be used in all of these types of programs.

Psychiatric rehabilitation is an approach that can be implemented across program models. The psychiatric rehabilitation approach has been implemented, for example, in supported education programs (Sul-

Table 2—The Three Phases of the Psychiatric Rehabilitation Process

PHASE	ACTIVITIES
Diagnosing	**Assessing rehabilitation readiness**
	Developing rehabilitation readiness
	Setting an overall rehabilitation goal • Connecting with clients • Identifying personal criteria • Describing alternative environments • Choosing the goal
	Functional assessment • Listing critical skills • Describing skill use • Evaluating skill functioning • Coaching the client
	Resource assessment • Listing critical resources • Describing resource use • Evaluating resource use • Coaching the client
Planning	**Planning for skills development** • Setting priorities • Defining objectives • Choosing interventions • Formulating the plan
	Planning for resource development • Setting priorities • Defining objectives • Choosing interventions • Formulating the plan

(continued)

Table 2—The Three Phases of the Psychiatric Rehabilitation Process *(continued)*

PHASE	ACTIVITIES
Intervening	**Direct skills teaching** • Outlining skill content • Planning the lesson • Coaching the client **Skills use programming** • Identifying barriers • Developing the program • Supporting client action **Resource coordination** • Marketing clients to resources • Problem solving • Programming resource use **Resource modification** • Assessing readiness for change • Proposing change • Consulting to resources • Training resources

From Anthony, W. A., Cohen, M. R., Farkas, M. D., & Gagne, C. (2001). *Psychiatric rehabilitation (2nd ed.).* Boston MA: Boston University, Center for Psychiatric Rehabilitation.

---

livan, Nicolellis, Danley & MacDonald-Wilson, 1993), supported employment programs (Danley, Sciarappa & MacDonald-Wilson, 1992), day treatment centers (Drake, Becker, Biesanz, Torrey, McHugo & Wyzik, 1994), clubhouses (Tayler, Piagesi, McNaught & Nielson, 1987), and PACT case management teams (Kramer, Anthony, Rogers & Kennard, 1999).

The host organization does need to have a philosophy and a set of values that are compatible with those of the approach (see Table 1) for optimal integration to occur. A program using the psychiatric rehabilitation approach incorporates a set of activities reflecting the psychiatric

Table 3—Comprehensive Array of Mental Health Services

Mission: Recovery

MENTAL HEALTH SERVICES (and Outcomes)	IMPACT OF SEVERE MENTAL ILLNESS		
	Impairment (Disorder in Thought, Feelings, and Behavior)	**Disability** (Role Performance Limited)	**Disadvantage** (Opportunity Restrictions)
Treatment (Symptom Relief)	✓		
Crises Intervention (Safety)	✓		
Case Management (Access)	✓	✓	✓
Rehabilitation (Role Functioning)		✓	✓
Enrichment (Self-Development)		✓	✓
Rights Protection (Equal Opportunity)			✓
Basic Support (Survival)			✓
Self-Help (Empowerment)		✓	✓
Wellness (Health)	✓		

Adapted from Anthony, W. A., Cohen, M. R., Farkas, M. D., & Gagne, C. (2001). *Psychiatric rehabilitation (2nd ed.).* Boston MA: Boston University, Center for Psychiatric Rehabilitation; Anthony, W. A. (1993). Recovery from mental illness: The guiding vision of the mental health service system in the 1990s. *Psychosocial Rehabilitation Journal, 16,* 11–23.

rehabilitation process. The program will typically have a specific set of policies, activities, record-keeping systems, and quality assurance mechanisms that facilitate the process. For example, important cornerstones of the rehabilitation process include the tasks of identifying what is important to the individual in making a choice, researching what alternatives exist, and following a set of structured steps to actually make a choice of preferred roles. Therefore, these will become specific tasks for certain personnel, records will be kept reflecting these tasks, activities will be organized to increase success in completing these tasks, and supervision will be conducted to ensure that the personnel and the activities are helping the person achieve the desired result. Examples of such programs include the "Choose-Get-Keep" program (Anthony et al., 2001) and the Role Recovery program (Anthony et al., 2001).

> **The process of Rehabilitation Readiness is designed to help consumers feel more confidant, aware, and committed to their rehabilitation.**

Psychotherapy done with people who have serious psychiatric disabilities or impairment is not, per se, psychiatric rehabilitation. While therapy is often useful and important, it is not the same as psychiatric rehabilitation. Specific techniques, such as skills training or psychoeducation for the family are also not equivalent to psychiatric rehabilitation, although such techniques can be useful in an overall psychiatric rehabilitation approach.

> **Psychiatric rehabilitation is a complex approach with a specific philosophy, a set of values and a defined process that results in a person with serious psychiatric disability being able to select, obtain, and maintain a valued role as a full citizen in society.**

In summary, psychiatric rehabilitation is a complex approach with a specific philosophy, a set of values, and a defined process that results in a person with serious psychiatric disability being able to select, obtain, and maintain a valued role as a full citizen in society. It is one service in an array of services dedicated to the overall mission of recovery.

CHAPTER *2* Description of Rehabilitation Readiness

INTRODUCTION

This chapter clarifies the intended meaning of Rehabilitation Readiness, identifies the different types of Rehabilitation Readiness, describes the basic assumptions underlying Rehabilitation Readiness, and explains the indicators of readiness used in the assessment of Rehabilitation Readiness.

Rehabilitation readiness enables both the client and the practitioner to decide if the client is, in fact, prepared for the arduous process of change involved in rehabilitation (Cohen et al., 1997). Both recovery and rehabilitation imply growth.

> **Rehabilitation, like recovery, requires courage, persistence, the willingness to hope again, and the willingness to accept setbacks and to rise yet again while working towards a goal.**

Rehabilitation, like recovery, requires courage, persistence, the willingness to hope again, and the willingness to accept setbacks and to rise yet again while working towards a goal. There are different types of readiness to consider over the course of the rehabilitation process: readiness for rehabilitation change; readiness to engage in a specific program or with a specific helper; and readiness to continue the ongoing process of rehabilitation.

TYPES OF READINESS

Readiness for Change

People vary in their willingness to confront change of any kind (Prochaska, Velicer, DiClemente & Fava, 1988; McConnaughy,

DiClemente, Prochaska & Velicer, 1989; Snow, Prochaska & Rossi, 1992). Some are more willing to stay in an unsatisfying situation and suffer, than to strike out and make a change. Others have no tolerance for discomfort and seek change immediately. People vary in their willingness to take action in relation to a needed or desired change (Norcross & Prochaska, 1986; Prochaska, DiClemente & Norcross, 1992).

In addition to individual variations in their eagerness for change in general, people also vary in their willingness to contemplate the types of changes implied in the psychiatric rehabilitation process. The process of psychiatric rehabilitation focuses on gaining or improving a valued role. This focus may challenge people to make behavioral or lifestyle changes. A person may begin to talk about the roles he or she desires and may discover that the desired role requires many changes

> From the consumer's perspective, past failures, the daunting challenge of overcoming symptoms, stigma, inertia, and aloneness can contribute to keeping many people from using rehabilitation.

that he or she has never even contemplated making. Changing from one role (e.g., clubhouse member) to another (e.g., history student) may require a person to process many changes simultaneously. For example, it may imply a change in identity, in social relationships, in the level of intellectual, physical, and/or emotional energy that the person is expected to bring to the new role, not to mention all the behavioral changes it may require.

Depending upon a person's readiness for change at a particular point in time, the reality of making a decision about what the future should bring (i.e., a job, a home, school, friends) and finding the will to do whatever it takes to make that choice, can be overwhelming. The state of readiness is not immutable, however, and often shifts with time. For example, entering into the rehabilitation process may be too great a change for someone to contemplate at the present time, but at a later time it may become more practicable and feasible.

The notion of readiness to change presents a formidable barrier—particularly when that change might result in regaining a real role in society again, or obtaining such a role for the first time. From the consumer's perspective, past failures, the daunting challenge of overcoming symptoms, stigma, inertia, and aloneness can contribute to keeping many people from using rehabilitation. Perhaps even more devastating, these barriers keep people from believing that real change is possible (Kramer & Gagne, 1996).

Readiness to Engage in a Specific Program or Agency

Regardless of how ready a person may be to make the necessary changes, that same person may or may not be ready to engage in a specific program. People have different ways in which they like to work. Some people like to work with a highly structured set of activities with explicit expectations for their participation. Other people prefer a more casual approach. Some like to work sporadically for long hours at a time and then not at all for several weeks. Others want to work for only an hour per week. People like to work with different kinds of helpers. Some like to work only with psychiatrists or psychologists. Others want to work only with fellow consumers. The characteristics of a particular program may or may not fit the preferred characteristics of the individual. Readiness to engage in a specific agency has been described more fully, particularly with respect to vocational goals in the *"Choose-Get-Keep" Approach to Employment Support: Intervention Manual* (Danley, 1997).

Readiness to Continue in an Ongoing Process

A third type of readiness relates to a person's readiness to continue the process he or she has undertaken. After exploring several options for a new role and setting, and understanding his or her own criteria for making a choice more fully, the individual may suddenly feel unable to continue. Fear of failing, fear of succeeding, or simply the fear of the unknown consequences of change can interfere insidiously and prevent a final choice. Such a crisis of confidence can occur at any stage of the rehabilitation or recovery process (Deegan, 1997; McCrory, Connolly, Hanson-Mayer, Sheridan-Landolfi, Barone, Blood, & Gilson, 1980; Spaniol, Gagne & Koehler, 1999). For example, a person may be considering returning to school and be completely overcome by the amount of time, money, and energy required to attend one class. Another student might be one semester away from graduation and be overwhelmed by the expectations of a "college graduate" that she perceives will soon be upon her. Consequently, readiness for change remains an issue throughout the process. The focus changes from a general readiness to commit to the rehabilitation process to the readiness for a specific activity within the process.

In summary, there are three types of readiness to consider: readiness for rehabilitation change; readiness to engage in a specific agency or type of agency, and readiness to continue. The skills and procedures described in training technology for Rehabilitation Readiness are focuses on the first type of readiness: the readiness to make the changes implied in rehabilitation process. They can, however, also be adapted for use with the other types of Rehabilitation Readiness.

THE PROCESS OF CHANGE

Prochaska and his colleagues are perhaps the best known proponents of a well-delineated approach to understanding the change process. In a comparative analysis of 24 models of psychotherapy, Prochaska and DiClemente (1984) concluded that there was good agreement across these widely differing models as to the processes that promote change. The model has described the process of change to predict behavior change across a wide range of both addictive and non-addictive problem behaviors (e.g., smoking and other problem health behaviors). According to this model, the modification of problem behavior involves progression through five stages: pre-contemplation, contemplation, preparation, action, and maintenance. While the progression is linear, an individual typically recycles through these stages several times before ending the problem behavior. Helping people progress through the stages involves matching particular processes and principles of change to particular stages of change.

Prochaska's Stages of Change
(Prochaska et al., 1992)

Pre-contemplation is the stage in which an individual has no intention to change the behavior in the near future. Others are often aware of a problem behavior or issue, but people at this stage are unaware or under-aware of their problems, and resist recognition of them.

Contemplation, the second stage, is the stage in which people are aware that a problem exists and are seriously thinking about doing something about it, but have not yet made a commitment to take action. They may not be ready to take action, and spend time weighing the pros and cons of the problem and its possible solutions. Individuals may stay in this stage for prolonged periods of time.

Preparation is the stage in which individuals are intending to take action in the next month and have taken action in the past year, but were unsuccessful.

Action is the stage in which individuals actually modify their behavior, experience, or environment in order to overcome their problem behavior. This stage is evidenced by significant overt behavioral changes and requires a considerable commitment of time and energy. The action stage is often mistakenly equated with change, so it is easy to overlook the prerequisite work that prepares people for action, or the subsequent stages that ensure maintenance of the changed behavior.

Maintenance is the stage in which people work to preserve the gains attained during action. It is a continuation of change, not the termination of the process, and is marked by stabilization of behavior change and avoiding relapse. Prochaska emphasizes that change continues even when the person has achieved his or her goal.

Rehabilitation Readiness and Prochaska's Model of Change

Prochaska's model of change has been discussed for mostly addictive behaviors (e.g., Blume & Schmaling, 1997; Hill, 1997; Prochaska, 1996; Prochaska, DiClemente, & Norcross, 1992; Silverstein, Hitzel, & Schenkel, 1998; Velicer, Rossi, DiClemente, & Prochaska, 1996). One study of a vocational rehabilitation intervention (Rogers, Martin,

Anthony, Massaro, Danley & Crean, in press) investigated the reliability of a change instrument that was based on Prochaska's model, (i.e., Change Assessment Scale by McConnaughy, Prochaska & Velicer, 1983) when used with a psychiatrically disabled population. As part of a larger vocational rehabilitation study, 242 participants with serious psychiatric disability, were asked to complete the instrument. Of the 163 participants who actually completed the instrument, 50% of subjects were seeking employment, and 23% wanted more education or training. Both of these expectations were consistent with the project's goals. When used with this population, the change instrument appeared to function similarly to the norm group of people with addictive behaviors. However, the precontemplation scores were somewhat higher among this group (indicating a lower readiness for change). Rogers and associates (in press) also found that the contemplation phase of change appeared to be more ambiguous for individuals with severe psychiatric disability. The authors suggest that the participants for the study had experienced repeated vocational failures which perhaps affected their responses to the instrument items.

The relationship of Prochaska's model of change to Rehabilitation Readiness is not clear at this time. Despite using the same term, "readiness," it seems that there are basic differences in the two approaches. Prochaska's model of change describes a process of change. In other words, he describes the stages that a person might go through as they move from not being ready for change of any kind to being ready for change. Rogers and associates' study suggests that the process of change may be the same for people with addictive behaviors and people with psychiatric disabilities, except for some variation in the pre-contemplation and contemplation phases. In contrast, Rehabilitation Readiness describes the elements or indicators that signal a person's willingness to *engage* in a rehabilitation process. It may be that Rehabilitation Readiness details out the indicators most relevant during the pre-contemplation and contemplation stages (the scales that showed the greatest differences between people with addictive behaviors and people with psychiatric disabilities) for beginning a specific type of action—that is, the setting of an overall rehabilitation goal.

REHABILITATION READINESS FOR CHANGE

There are five basic assumptions underlying Rehabilitation Readiness and the activities of Assessing and Developing Readiness (Table 4).

1. Readiness describes willingness and commitment to change, not capacity for change.

Readiness for rehabilitation is based on a number of indicators that reflect the person's preparedness to become actively involved in the rehabilitation process. Active involvement requires an interest in the process and a perception that rehabilitation will be useful. The desire to begin a rehabilitation process is based on perception and attitude rather than on capacity. An assessment of skill functioning and level of support is the appropriate mechanism to determine a person's capacity. Skill and support assessments are conducted as part of the rehabilitation process to determine what has to be done to help the person achieve a self-determined goal. Psychiatric rehabilitation organizes its interventions to facilitate the development of the person's capacity to achieve the goal that he or she has set. Readiness assessment focuses on the person's current willingness and preparedness to engage in that process.

Table 4— Assumptions Underlying Rehabilitation Readiness

1. Readiness describes willingness and commitment to change, not capacity for change.

2. Readiness changes over time.

3. Readiness is environmentally specific.

4. Readiness assessment involves the person during the process.

5. Readiness assessment is not intended to exclude people from the rehabilitation process.

2. Readiness changes over time.

Willingness to commit to change can vary over time. There are many changes in circumstances (e.g., economic, health, social, seasonal, geographic) that can contribute to changes in a person's feeling of willingness and his or her attitudes towards change itself. For example, some people feel a sense of hopefulness and energy in the spring that they do not feel in the winter. Readiness to change jobs, go on a trip, or engage in services may be more likely to occur in spring than in winter. For others, suddenly inheriting some money can lead to more or less readiness to change. For still others, the simple passing of time provides the chance to mull over the implications of what lies ahead and, again, can effect one's readiness to change. Readiness may change as often as every 4 to 6 weeks (Felton, Stastny, Shern, Blanch, Donahue, Knight, & Brown, 1995; Shern, Felton, Hough, Lehman, Goldfinger, Valencia, Dennis, Straw, & Wood, 1997). The assessment of readiness therefore describes only how open the person is to engaging in rehabilitation at the present time. The corollary to this assumption is that since readiness is not static, nor a personal trait, it can be facilitated or developed.

3. Readiness is environmentally specific.

Readiness varies not only over time but also across domains as well. The rehabilitation process focuses on one domain at a time: living (home/community), learning (school), or working (job). Readiness to take on the challenge of growth in one area is unrelated to readiness to take on the challenge in another area. For example, a person may be quite willing to begin the rehabilitation process of making changes in his or her living situation, yet that person may be totally unwilling to contemplate changes in his or her work situation. The assessment and development of readiness, therefore, has to focus on answering the question: "Am I prepared to commit myself to the rehabilitation process at this specific time with respect to this specific environment?"

4. Readiness assessment involves the person during the process.

Assessing and Developing Readiness procedures are designed to be used by the practitioner and client in partnership. The degree and timing of participation may vary depending on the client's willingness to participate and ability to participate fully, prior to a rehabilitation intervention. Some clients may be acutely ill at the time of the readiness assessment or may have just arrived in the service or agency for the first time. Time might be needed for orienting and engaging the person in some level of relationship before beginning to assess readiness. Other people in the same situation may be quite open and prepared to explore their readiness for rehabilitation. While some people may want and be able to collect or provide most of the information necessary for the assessment themselves, others may only want and be able to review the information that was collected by someone else. The practitioner, commensurate with general rehabilitation practice, must adapt the procedures to increase the client's participation. Regardless of the degree of participation in the assessment process, the client makes the final choice of service direction that follows the readiness assessment. Willingness to participate in readiness development activities increases the likelihood that the client will be able to use these activities to actually increase his or her willingness to participate in the whole rehabilitation process.

5. Readiness assessment is not intended to exclude people from the rehabilitation process.

Mandates seeking to shorten the amount of time spent in any one service, reduced service funding, and the lack of personnel trained in rehabilitation, all serve to pressure the mental health system into working only with those who are "ready" or "probably going to succeed." Assessment of readiness is not intended to create a new label for people with severe psychiatric disabilities (i.e., "ready" or "unready"). The label "unready" is often seen as code for "hard to work with." Programs are, therefore, sometimes tempted to exclude "unready" individuals or, at best, to create only maintenance oriented programs for people to pass the time. The concepts of readiness to change therefore risk being used by service systems as a way of meeting these service challenges.

Readiness assessment is intended to suggest only the next set of helpful activities that would be useful and desirable by the client. Clients who are not ready for rehabilitation at the present time may be ready at some other time. Programs that design readiness development activities can increase clients' current readiness.

Readiness assessment is not intended to exclude people from the rehabilitation process.

Readiness is assessed to help clients and practitioners or helpers to determine when and how best to begin the rehabilitation process.

The following chapters describe the elements of Assessing Readiness and Developing Readiness. The practitioner skills needed to conduct these activities are fully presented in two curricula: *Psychiatric Rehabilitation Training Technology: Assessing Readiness for Rehabilitation* (Farkas et al., 2000) and *Psychiatric Rehabilitation Training Technology: Developing Readiness for Rehabilitation* (Cohen, Forbess & Farkas, 2000).

CHAPTER 3 *Assessing Readiness for Rehabilitation*

INTRODUCTION

The central question of Assessing Readiness is whether or not the person is prepared, at a minimum, to successfully engage in the psychiatric rehabilitation process to select a preferred environment and to commit to the goal of being in the environment within or for the next 6 to 24 months. Engaging successfully in the goal-setting process means that the client not only completes that process in approximately 10 to 15 sessions, but also sets a meaningful goal that he or she intends to achieve. Assessing Readiness involves determining the extent to which the indicators of readiness are present.

READINESS INDICATORS

Readiness indicators are comprised of factors that influence the willingness to be engaged in the rehabilitation process. As Rogers and associates' (in press) found when studying Prochaska's change instrument, a person's diagnosis or level of pathology is not an indicator of readiness. While the person's response to his or her symptoms may, in fact, interfere with his or her desire to begin an involved, growth-oriented process at a particular moment in time, assessing the level of pathology does not provide specific information about readiness. People with the same diagnosis may differ greatly in their readiness to engage in a rehabilitation process. People with exactly the same symptom patterns may also differ greatly in their readiness to engage in a rehabilitation process (Blume & Schmaling, 1997; McConnaughy, DiClemente, Prochaska & Velicer, 1989).

**Table 5—Indicators for
Psychiatric Rehabilitation Readiness**

Need for Change
Commitment to Change
Personal Closeness
Self-Awareness
Environmental Awareness

There are five indicators that influence willingness to become involved in the rehabilitation process (Table 5). These include:

1. Need for Change, or the extent to which a person is either unsuccessful or unsatisfied in his or her current situation;

2. Commitment to Change or the extent to which a person is committed to make changes in his or her life;

3. Personal Closeness or the extent to which he or she is open to connecting with others;

4. Self-Awareness or the extent to which the person has some level of understanding about himself or herself; and lastly,

5. Environmental Awareness or the degree to which a person is aware of the differences between environments.

Need for Change

The need to make a change arises from two possible pressures. The first is the person's own perceptions about his or her lack of success and/or satisfaction with the current situation. The second is external pressure to improve functioning or change environments.

Martin, Rogers & Farkas (1999) reviewed the literature about the correlates of an individual's perception of satisfaction. A perception of satisfaction appears to be related to the degree of congruence between the individual's needs, capabilities, and aspirations; and the resources, demands, and opportunities characteristic of the environment (Kalman, 1983). Evidence exists to suggest that the match between the person and the environment has a considerable role in determining outcomes both in residential and vocational environments (Holland, 1985; Segal, Silverman & Baumohl, 1989; Thompson, Flynn & Griffith, 1994). Internal pressure for change comes from some degree of dissatisfaction with the current situation. The current situation is defined as the person's role and setting in the domain of greatest dissatisfaction (e.g., residential, vocational, educational). The process of Assessing Readiness (Farkas et al., 2000) begins with a structured interview exploring the individual's degree of dissatisfaction. At times, a person may be unwilling to express dissatisfaction with the environment. The person may follow all the rules of the environment, make no complaints, and do whatever is asked, but do this out of fear of the consequences of truly expressing dissatisfaction. The practitioner's skills are key to gaining the trust necessary for clients to feel safe enough to explore their actual degree of satisfaction or dissatisfaction.

External pressure comes from the dissatisfaction of those who are important in the current environment. These are typically the "gatekeepers" in an environment or the people who can greatly influence the decision to allow the person to remain in their current situation. "Gatekeepers" are those with implicit or explicit organizational or group authority in the environment (Chase & Bell, 1990; McClellan, 1974; Scott, Balch & Flynn, 1985; Wallston, Hoover-Dempsey, Brissie & Rozee-Koker, 1989). For example, they may include work supervisors, work team leaders, administrators, teachers, mentors, principals, parents, elder siblings, and mental health or rehabilitation professionals. Besides gatekeepers, others who are relevant to the process are those people who can greatly influence the individual or the environment's perception of a person's success in a particular environment. These are often referred to as "significant others." Parents may be significant others, as well as important gatekeepers in the living situation, because they have an important influence on the individual and also have the power to decide whether the person can stay or will have to leave their home. These same parents, while playing a role as significant others in the residential environment, may not be relevant as gatekeepers when the area in question is, for example, that of work. Supervisors, co-workers or bosses are usually the gatekeepers at work. External pressure for change can also arise when rules or policies change (e.g., time limits, closings, and space limitations). In this situation, the pressure comes from the institution or the organization as a whole, rather than coming from particular individuals.

The need to become involved in rehabilitation is based on the need to improve the person's satisfaction and/or to meet an environmental demand. It is difficult to proceed with rehabilitation if there is only external pressure for change and no internal pressure for change. For

Need, like readiness, is specific to a point in time. While there might be no pressure for rehabilitation at one point in time, circumstances or the person's feelings might change to create the need at a different point in time

example, a person may be living quite happily at home with his or her family, while the family may be unhappy with the way in which the person is behaving in the home. They may complain often, both to the person and to the practitioner. The family may not, however, be sufficiently unhappy to ask the person to leave. In this situation, the person may have difficulty experiencing the need for rehabilitation until a clear crisis occurs. When the external pressure results in the person having to move to another environment, rehabilitation becomes a relevant issue. For example, if someone loses his or her job, there will be an immediate change of environment regardless of the person's own desires or perceptions about the job. The change will result in having to make a choice about whether to stay unemployed or to get a new job. The issue of whether or not the person is prepared to make such a choice, and thus the process of Rehabilitation Readiness itself becomes relevant, regardless of the fact that the pressure was strictly external.

If the gatekeepers or influential people in an environment see the person as successful, and the person is satisfied, there is no immediate need for rehabilitation. At times, practitioner's views about the quality of life led by the client are in direct conflict with the perceptions of the client and the gatekeepers of the current environment. For example, a person may be living in what is perceived by the practitioner to be unacceptable conditions. If the person is satisfied with the standard of living and the landlord is satisfied with the person living there, there is no immediate pressure, or need for rehabilitation. The client may, at some point in the future, come to the conclusion that this living situation is unsatisfactory. Equally, the landlord may, at some point, decide to terminate the lease. In either case, there will then be a need for rehabilitation.

In summary, the need for rehabilitation exists if either the client or the important people in the environment are dissatisfied with the client being in the current situation. Need, like readiness, is specific to a point in time. While there might be no pressure for rehabilitation at one point in time, circumstances or the person's feelings might change to create the need at a different point in time. If there is no need established, investigating other readiness indicators has no meaning and therefore, the assessment of readiness is terminated for the time being.

Commitment to Change

The need to engage in a change process is different from the desire to engage in a change process. People are often willing to endure the unhappiness they have, rather than face the unpredictable implications of making a change. While a person may be unhappy in the current environment and wish to change, he or she may feel unable to seriously contemplate making a change because of a belief that any new situation would be too much to handle.

Motivation or the lack of motivation has often been associated with a diagnosis of major mental illness (Geczy & Sultenfuss, 1995; Anderson & Lewis, 1999; Kelly, van Kammen & Allen; 1999). In many service settings, the lack of progress in a helping intervention has been attributed to the "client's lack of motivation" or "treatment resistance," which can become a static label attached to the client, rather than a signal to investigate further (Anthony et al., 1990). The rehabilitation process makes the assumption that there are many factors that contribute to motivation.

> The term *commitment to change* is used rather than *motivation* as a way of shifting the focus to the notion of active involvement by the client, rather than a symptom that the client cannot control.

Rather than viewing lack of motivation as a negative symptom, rehabilitation seeks to understand the internal and external factors that may contribute to a person's motivation to participate in helping interventions.

The term *commitment to change* is used rather than *motivation* as a way of shifting the focus to the notion of active involvement by the client, rather than a symptom that the client cannot control. The indicator, Commitment to Change, reflects the person's intention to change, (i.e., improve his or her functioning or to change the environment). The central questions the person needs to answer in determining how much he or she may want to change are: Does change seem possible? Does the change seem desirable? A person's commitment to change is influenced by whether the person has successfully made changes in the past, the person's expectations about the difficulty of making changes, and his or her level of confidence about being able to manage the change.

> A person's commitment to change is influenced by whether the person has successfully made changes in the past, the person's expectations about the difficulty of making changes, and his or her level of confidence about being able to manage the change.

Some people have had many failures in the past and have little hope that anything will be different in the future, no matter how hard they try. Others feel incapable of managing the stress that accompanies change, fearing a possible increase or return of symptoms. Studies confirm that positive expectations and perceptions about one's ability to have an important impact on the environment affects behavior and task performance (Gold, 1990). A perceived inability to influence one's environment has been tied to significant performance deficits (Hiroto & Seligman, 1975).

Bandura (1997) describes the complexities of self-efficacy as a belief about one's own ability to influence the environment that impacts on the person's desire to try new experiences or work until mastery occurs. This desire occurs independent of the level of skill the person possesses. Self-efficacy theory is based on the principle that cognitive processes can affect behavioral change and that cognition is altered by the person's experience of mastery (Bandura, 1977). How a person understands the reasons for success, in other words, plays a larger role in sustaining a person's effort over time than that person's actual ability (Weiner, 1985). For example, people who believe that they failed because they did not work hard enough are likely to work harder the next time, whereas people who believe that they failed because of circumstances or a lack of ability are likely to give up more easily. This is particularly true of those for whom ability represents a stable, internal attribute, rather than a behavior that can be mastered (Bandura, 1997). The more a person's explanations about success and failure in a situation are tied to a belief in his or her own efficacy, the more successful the person becomes in the future (Relich, Debus & Walker, 1986; Schunk & Gunn, 1985).

The client's experience of how much others' support the rehabilitation process itself also influences how willing the client will be to enter into rehabilitation. Setting and achieving a personal goal is a lengthy, and at times, arduous process. The support of significant others helps the client to take the first step and to continue working with the rehabilitation process, once it has begun. The kind of support of significant others that is critical in this phase of the rehabilitation process is different from the specific support or resources the client might

> The client's experience of how much others' support the rehabilitation process itself also influences how willing the client will be to enter into rehabilitation.

need to achieve the goal. The perception of support is more important than the actual support itself during the assessment of readiness. The extent to which a client feels he can count on his family members to give him a ride to the rehabilitation agency on a regular basis is an example of the kind of support that impacts on the person's commitment to change. In contrast, a client might need the support of his case manager to wake him up in the morning to go to school. That specific support allows the client to succeed in his specific overall rehabilitation goal of completing his education. The support of significant others with respect to the client making some change in his or her life, gives the client more confidence about the decision to enter into the rehabilitation process (Wallston et al., 1989).

The information relevant to this support includes an understanding of who the client perceives to be his or her "significant others," what the support is that the client wants, and the client's perception of the significant other's willingness to provide the support. Beels (1981) maintains that social support networks may be based to a varying extent on family, friends, neighbors, work mates, fellow consumers, or members of a group or church. For any individual, different aspects of the network may be important at different times for different purposes. The support dimension is influenced by the person's conceptions about the desirability of receiving support from significant others, and his or her expectations of their commitment. A study by Lee, Lieh-Mak and Spinks (1993) of the coping strategies of 101 people with schizophrenia, found that the more experience clients had with sources of help, the better the outcomes. In addition, the person's motivation and use of available helpful sources was an important mediator of outcome.

People differ in terms of their connectedness to other people. For those who like and want relationships, it is crucial that the people they view as most important in their lives are willing to provide the backing they want for their participation in rehabilitation. For these clients, support is essential to their motivation to both begin and persist in completing the rehabilitation process. For others, who are less open to relationships and who are less interested in being close to others, the support indicator is not as critical to their willingness to begin the process. However, support may become more important to completing the process once the person becomes engaged with a practitioner, and over time, begins to experience the benefits of feeling supported.

Personal Closeness

First person accounts of the recovery process indicate that the consumer-survivors identify the presence of another person, "just being there," as one of the most important factors in their success (Deegan, 1988). Making a change may appear more feasible in the presence of a strong relationship with at least one person, preferably a helping practitioner or peer of some kind, in order to withstand the stress and fears that arise during the course of the rehabilitation process. The indicator, Personal Closeness refers to the person's willingness to form a personal connection with another. Some people are content with having limited personal relationships. Others enjoy being close to many other people. A person's willingness to form a personal connection, therefore, can range from being open to personal closeness to being closed and desirous of isolation. A person who is open to relationships is more likely to experience support and receive general support from others. Therefore, a person who is open to personal closeness is more likely to be willing to sustain the process of rehabilitation over time.

Studies report that the client's perception of the relationship is a consistent predictor of improvement (Bachelor, 1995). Studies by Wasylenki, Goering, Lancee, Ballantyne & Farkas, 1988) provide evidence of the positive effects of the rehabilitation practitioner-client relationship in psychiatric rehabilitation. They found that client satisfaction with the relationship was an important factor in promoting positive outcomes. A more recent study by Gehrs & Goering (1994) examined further the association between the quality of the "working alliance" and rehabilitation outcomes. In this study the client's (as well as the practitioner's) perception of the quality of the working alliance were significantly correlated with outcomes. The client's perception of the quality of the relationship may have something to do with his or her openness to having relationships at all. Some authors feel that the client's collaboration, as distinct from the practitioner's, is the essence of what is effective in any helping process (Frieswyk et al., 1986; Colson, 1986). Research suggests that the working alliance is a result of the interaction and match of the client's relationship style and the practitioner's relationship style (Tyrell, Dozier, Teague & Fallot, 1999).

> **First person accounts of the recovery process indicate that the consumer-survivors identify the presence of another person, "just being there," as one of the most important factors in their success.**

In order to understand a person's openness to personal closeness, it is important to assess his or her personal style of relating as well as the actual degree to which the person is connected to others in their life (Tyrell, Dozier, Teague & Fallot, 1999). "Personal styles of relating" refer to the domain through which the person usually develops closeness with others: physical, intellectual, emotional, or spiritual (Carkhuff, 1981; Egan, 1994). A preference for relating through physical closeness is demonstrated by the person choosing physical activities or tasks to do with another person as their primary means of developing the bonds of a relationship. For example, some people prefer to play a sport or watch a sport on television with others as a way of furthering their relationships with others. Others feel the closest to those with whom they can discuss the behaviors and emotional reactions of others. Still others prefer to engage in heated intellectual debate, with no direct emotional content. Two people with an intellectual style can argue about world affairs and feel that the person with whom they are arguing is their best friend. Still others feel that they are in a close relationship with another if they share an exploration and profession of spiritual belief.

If a person who prefers to develop a relationship based upon physical activities is matched with a helping person whose preference is for intellectual or emotional closeness, the relationship will be slow to develop, if it develops at all. Further, the helping person can make the error of judging the client whose personal style is different from his or her own style, as someone who does not want or like personal closeness at all. This is particularly true if the helping person has no other opportunities to observe the client in interaction. Assessing a person's preferential style is an important clue to understanding where to look to find out how likely that person may be to want to engage in a close relationship during the rehabilitation process.

The assessment of readiness implies that there is some openness to personal closeness at the outset in order for the process to be conducted in a truly interactive way. If, however, the degree of openness is minimal and the person prefers distance rather than closeness, the helper or practitioner can choose to stop the assessment process and spend time engaging the client in the partnership. Alternatively, the practitioner can work with the minimal closeness and try to engage the person in small parts of the assessment process over time.

Awareness

Awareness of self and the environment are the next two indicators of Rehabilitation Readiness. Both types of awareness help the client set the overall rehabilitation goal without intensive educational development. Awareness is more of an intellectual factor while Need, Commitment to Change, and Personal Closeness are more emotionally based. Awareness is a function of both the client's knowledge and his or her experience in the world.

Self-Awareness

Self-awareness is a complex factor that has been much discussed across several disciplines, especially as it relates to people with a psychiatric disability (Ferrari & Sternberg, 1998; Amador & David, 1998; DeHoff, 1998). Synthesis of the concept of self-awareness reveals that a person's level of self-awareness is influenced by how well the person has processed internal experiences, especially major decisions and reactions to major life. People differ in terms of their level of introspection. Some are highly attuned to how they are experiencing events. They are very interested in themselves and enjoy learning about themselves. Others avoid introspection. They may be highly sensitive to external stimuli and unable to process their strong internal reactions. Painful experiences may have taught them to cut off their emotional responses.

> When clients have self-awareness, it is easier to engage them in the rehabilitation process.

When clients have self-awareness, it is easier to engage them in the rehabilitation process. They are able to contribute their interests, values, and personal preferences to the goal-setting process. Those who are self-aware are also often willing to acknowledge their skill strengths and deficits and are often interested in further development of their skills.

The onset of disability can exert a major influence on one's values, interests, personal preferences, and world view, typically requiring a restructuring of that value system (Kelly, Keany & Glueckauf, 1993). This realignment of the value system may occur because the person's pre-disability values, interests, and personal preferences are no longer applicable. For persons with psychiatric disability, the basic values may not change, but the person's belief in the possibility of fulfilling them may radically change. The degree to which the client is clear about his or her current values reflects one part of the important self-knowledge that allows full participation in the rehabilitation process.

Environmental Awareness

The entire rehabilitation process is based on the fit between the person and the environment. Psychiatric rehabilitation goal setting identifies the environment that the client wants. Functional and resource assessment determine the skills and resources that are both demanded by the goal environment and wanted by the client. Skill and resource development help the client to respond to the specific demands of the goal environment. Environmental Awareness, or having an understanding about environments is a critical component in the rehabilitation process (Segal et al., 1989; Farkas et al., 1989; Anthony et al., 1990).

The information relevant to environmental awareness includes knowledge about the differences in the people, the activities, and the physical setting, in a variety of environments. The person's environmental awareness is influenced by the amount of the person's experience in different environments and his or her interest in learning about different environments through reading and speaking with others. Some familiarity with the different types of residential, education, vocational, and social) settings is necessary to formulate an image of a future environment. The image of there being a "better" environment somewhere motivates the client to begin the rehabilitation process. A person's ideas about possible future roles have a powerful effect on his or her current motivation.

> The entire rehabilitation process is based on the fit between the person and the environment.

According to Markus and Nurius (1986), the majority of daily activities may not be linked to the current view of the self, but what may be possible in the future. Environmental awareness contributes to a person's sense of possibilities. When a person understands the variety and the nature of the roles and settings that are in the arena that he or she is interested in or concerned about, that concrete understanding may help that person lose preconceived notions that contributed to his or her feelings of entrapment, resignation, and defeat.

In summary, Assessing Readiness is determining how willing a person is to engage in rehabilitation. The extent to which a person is currently viewed as unsuccessful or feels unhappy (Need); sees change as possible and positive (Commitment to Change); is at least somewhat open to connecting with others (Personal Closeness); understands his or her own interests, values, styles of decision making (Self-Awareness) and knows something about the characteristics of the types of environments that exist in the domain of his or her concern (Environmental Awareness) all provide an indication of how willing the person may be to begin the rehabilitation process. The aim of Assessing Readiness is to reach a mutual understanding about what the next activities should be.

CHOOSING A DIRECTION

Since rehabilitation rests on a partnership between the practitioner and client, the client selects the strategy for moving ahead, at the end of the readiness assessment process. The strategy chosen depends upon whether the client's overall profile of readiness indicates that he or she is currently ready to begin rehabilitation and the extent to which the client is interested in the rehabilitation process.

For clients whose ratings seem to suggest that they are sufficiently prepared to begin the rehabilitation process, the strategy for moving ahead is to begin the activity of Setting an Overall Rehabilitation Goal (Cohen et al., 1991). At times, the assessment ratings will be equivocal and the strategy is selected based on the client's interest. If the client is enthusiastic about figuring out where he or she wants to live, learn, or work over the next 6 to 24 months, the overall rehabilitation goal-setting process is appropriate. The practitioner may work with the client to increase his or her preparedness along some of the indicators, which scored low during the assessment.

For those whose ratings suggest that it would be helpful to pursue an alternative to beginning with the rehabilitation process at the current

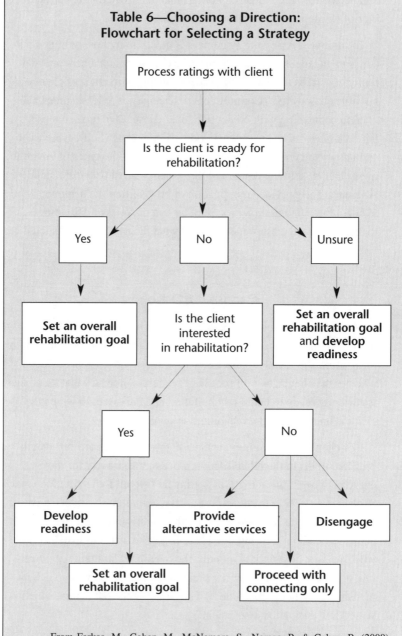

**Table 6—Choosing a Direction:
Flowchart for Selecting a Strategy**

From Farkas, M., Cohen, M., McNamara, S., Nemec, P., & Cohen, B. (2000). *Psychiatric rehabilitation training technology: Assessing readiness for rehabilitation.* Boston, MA: Boston University, Center for Psychiatric Rehabilitation.

time, other choices include: to develop readiness, to link with other services, to maintain personal contact, or to disengage from services.

Linking with Other Services

Choosing to link with another service can imply that the client and the practitioner feel that issues other than rehabilitation are the ones that the client wants to focus on at this point in time (for example by engaging in treatment services). It can mean that the client feels that the structured process of rehabilitation is too demanding at this time and she would prefer to link with self-help or enrichment services. Linking to other services involves further exploration by the client and practitioner. Often information gathered during the readiness assessment suggests which other services might be more urgent or desirable for the client at the current time.

> If the only choice a person can make is to engage with the mental health system, then there is no choice.

Maintaining Personal Contact

Choosing to only maintain personal contact implies that while the client is willing for the practitioner to call or drop in on a regular basis, the client feels unwilling to receive any other formal service at the present time. Maintaining personal contact means that the practitioner uses his or her connecting skills to strengthen the relationship with the client and continues to informally assess changes in the client's readiness for rehabilitation.

Disengaging

Choosing to disengage from any service is another possible direction. Disengaging or terminating from services should be expected. People disengage from services when they don't see the service as sufficiently beneficial at this time. Regardless of the reason for disengagement, it is important for consumers to have the opportunity to review and reflect on their experiences using the service. Disengagement is an opportunity for consumers and practitioners to consolidate what they have learned from their work together (Danley, 1997). Disengagement is often the most difficult choice for a practitioner or helper to support. "Allowing" the client to disengage can be viewed by the practitioner to be an abandonment of the client. The practitioner can see the client's decision to disengage as the result of the client's presumed, impaired decision-making capacity which would then again necessitate a practitioner intervention.

A true choice, however, must have at least two options. If the only choice a person can make is to engage with the mental health system, then there is no choice. Supporting the client's wish to disengage does not mean that the practitioner closes his or her door. It means that the person does not see himself or herself as wanting or needing any of the offered services at this time. In supporting the informed choice of disengagement, the practitioner helps the individual to evaluate his or her experiences with the service to date and skillfully terminates the relationship. The practitioner may also review with the consumer how the re-engagement process can happen if the consumer desires it in the future.

CHAPTER *4* *Developing Readiness for Rehabilitation*

INTRODUCTION

Based on the results of the readiness assessment, the client may choose to develop readiness for rehabilitation before an setting the overall rehabilitation goal. When the client is interested in the idea of rehabilitation and understands his or her current lack of readiness, the activities of Developing Readiness help the individual to increase his or her willingness to engage in the rehabilitation process. The Developing Readiness strategy empowers the person to engage in rehabilitation, with the belief that it will improve his or her life. Developing Readiness can aid in the person's recovery process as well, in that it usually results in the person acquiring a broader, more hopeful view of himself or herself and the possibility of regaining a valued role.

This chapter will provide an overview of Developing Readiness. Developing Readiness overcomes the barriers to readiness that are represented by the low ratings on readiness indicators. Readiness assessment is prescriptive in that it points to areas that would be helpful for the client to develop, to increase his or her preparedness for rehabilitation. Understanding a client's readiness to make a change and appreciating barriers to change can improve client satisfaction and lower both client and practitioner frustration during the change process (Zimmerman, Olsen & Bosworth, 2000). To increase the degree to which the person is prepared for the lengthy process of rehabilitation, the practitioner creates new experiences that are designed to help the person develop a different perspective on his or her rehabilitation. By increasing the client's exposure to motivating activities, clarifying any

> **Developing Readiness provides opportunities for the client to learn and grow beyond his or her current view of the potential for change.**

personal implications derived from the client's circumstances or exposure to these activities, and demonstrating to the client that she or he has credible support, the client is more likely to view the change process of rehabilitation as desirable, possible, and manageable (Cohen et al., 2000).

Increasing a client's exposure to activities that help the client to increase his or her understanding of self, recovery, alternative environments, and rehabilitation can motivate the individual to commit to the rehabilitation process. A client's life's circumstances may have limited his experience or exposure to recovery and rehabilitation. He may have not have had the opportunities to process his feelings and experiences and therefore develop insight about himself or his recovery. The focus of organizing motivational activities is to change a person's attitudes, as opposed to changing a person's behavior.

After participating in a variety of motivational activities, the client then needs to be able to clarify the personal implications from the motivating activities (Cohen, Forbess et al, 2000). Clarifying personal implications helps the client understand new insights and recognize the consequences of the insights for his or her readiness to rehabilitation. It involves processing the knowledge gained from motivational activities and personalizing it.

Both group and individual activities to develop readiness are described in *Psychiatric Rehabilitation Practitioner Tools: Developing Readiness* (BCPR, Consulting Inc., 2001).

The last activity of Developing Readiness is demonstrating credible support (Cohen, Forbess & Farkas, 2000). The client needs to know that she is not facing rehabilitation alone. After developing insight and before making any changes, the client needs to feel that family, friends, helpers, and other significant others will be there for her as she embarks on rehabilitation or recovery activities.

Developing Readiness provides opportunities for the client to learn and grow beyond his or her current view of the potential for change. For example, a client and practitioner may agree that the client is not ready to set a rehabilitation goal in the work environment because the client has very limited experience and knowledge of alternative work environments. In Developing Readiness, the client and practitioner create opportunities for the client to learn more about work environments. Attending a job fair, visiting a variety of work environments, reading about work environments, and participating in a work program at a psychosocial clubhouse are a few of the many possible activities that will increase the client's awareness of alternative work environments. During and after these motivational activities, the practitioner and client discuss the client's experiences.

IMPLICATIONS OF READINESS RATINGS FOR DEVELOPING READINESS

Developing Need

A low rating on the indicator of Need for Change does not usually lead to the activity of Developing Readiness but rather leads to terminating the readiness assessment process. A low rating on this indicator generally means that the person is satisfied and successful in his or her current environment and believes that there is no need for rehabilitation, either to change environment or to improve functioning in the environment. People, who are satisfied with the way things are and are not being pressured to make a change, would most likely choose a different strategy than rehabilitation. They may choose not to continue the readiness assessment. They may choose to disengage from any helping service. Recent studies support this tendency, using Prochaska's Transtheoretical, or Stages of Change Model (Prochaska et al., 1992), as a measure of readiness. Brown, Melchior, Panter, Slaughter & Huba (2000), investigating 451 women with substance abuse issues, proposed that the subjects' readiness to seek help was related to the time urgency or pressure of their treatment issues. A second study of 181 pre-treatment clients at an outpatient community mental health center showed similar results (Walker, 1999). Clients in the earlier

> The focus of organizing motivational activities is to change a person's attitudes, as opposed to changing a person's behavior.

stages of change (i.e., pre-contemplation or contemplation) showed significantly less motivational distress (anxiety, global distress, and depression) than clients with advanced profiles for readiness for change. In the language of readiness assessment, the clients were less dissatisfied with their current situation and thus had less need for rehabilitation.

There are several common barriers to Rehabilitation Readiness, however, that could affect the indicator of Need. If the person who rated low on Need during the readiness assessment was interested in rehabilitation anyway, Developing Readiness may still be appropriate. If the rating of Need was high due to the fact that significant others perceived the person as highly unsuccessful and likely to be asked to leave his current situation, then further exploring the reasons for the person's perceptions of satisfaction with his current environment may be appropriate. A lack of self-understanding could lead someone to misrate his or her current level of success and satisfaction. A lack of understanding of recovery and its implications may affect the rating on Need. If a person has low expectations about what is possible in life, she may be very satisfied with a difficult situation, thinking that the current situation is "as good as it gets." Similarly, a lack of understanding about alternative environments might lower her feelings of dissatisfaction with what she has. If a person does not really understand what the alternatives to the current environment could potentially be, she will not know what she is missing. Consequently, she may be more satisfied with the current situation than she would otherwise be. Increasing a person's dissatisfaction with the current situation through motivational activities might include listening to or reading speakers describe their recovery experiences, hearing objective facts and information, or discussing consequences of behaviors. To the extent that these activities increase the person's dissatisfaction, there will be an increase in a sense of need for rehabilitation.

Developing Commitment to Change

Low ratings on Commitment to Change can stem from any of the following areas explored during the readiness assessment: desire, positive expectations, self-efficacy and/or support. The extent to which a person understands the possibilities of recovery, the stages of recovery, the role of the practitioner in psychiatric rehabilitation, the components of the psychiatric rehabilitation process, and exactly what she will be engaged in when she begins the process, affects that person's desire for change. Understanding psychiatric rehabilitation also helps the client to identify the kinds of outcomes that are possible using this approach and therefore helps the client to clarify any expectations of what change might bring. Because motivation is largely, although not only, a cognitive construct (Bandura, 1977), increasing a client's understanding of recovery, rehabilitation, and possible positive outcomes strengthens the individual's motivation for change.

A low rating on Commitment to Change could mean that the person is either consciously or unconsciously ignoring the need to change (lack of desire), or at least not paying it full attention. Bandura's (1986) social cognitive theory, among others (e.g., Prochaska et al., 1992; Janis & Mann, 1977), describes inattention as a means of blocking or processing potentially motivating information. Clarifying the personal implications of a person's experiences through cognitive therapy, counseling, peer support groups or "walk and talk" groups, can be helpful in overcoming such inattention. "Walk and talk" groups are groups of two or more consumers who literally go for walks and talk about important issues while they are walking. Such groups are useful in developing a desire for change for those who feel that physical activity is an important way of connecting with others.

Low ratings on Commitment to Change may be a function of motivational activities not matching the individual's stage of readiness to change. Prochaska and Prochaska write:

> Clients in the pre-contemplative stage typically cannot change without special help. Those in the contemplation stage are not sure they want to change [or desire, in rehabilitation readiness terms]. Those in the preparation stage are afraid they do not know how to successfully change [lack of positive expectations or self efficacy in rehabilitation readiness terms]. The levels of change help guide therapists and clients on what to change. (Prochaska & Prochaska, 1999, p. 83).

Motivational activities need to be tailored to the individual's stage of motivational readiness, as findings from several recent studies in the area of health behavior change support (e.g., Annis, Schober & Kelly, 1996). A study by Marcus et al. (1998) of the efficacy of a tailored vs. a standard self-help physical activity intervention at the workplace revealed that those receiving the motivationally tailored intervention were significantly more likely to show increases and less likely to show either no change or regression in stage of motivational readiness. In addition, changes in stage of motivational readiness were significantly associated with changes in self-reported time spent in exercise. Borsari and Carey (2000) did a randomized

> **The idea of motivational tailoring suggests that to successfully develop readiness for rehabilitation, it is important to understand how much someone wants to change as well as how that individual wants or can use the help delivered, to do it.**

controlled trial of a 1-session motivational intervention for 60 college student binge drinkers at Syracuse University. The brief intervention group provided 30 of the students with feedback regarding personal consumption, perceived drinking norms, alcohol-related problems, situations associated with heavy drinking, and alcohol expectancies. The results revealed a significant reduction on the number of drinks consumed per week, number of times drinking alcohol in the past month, and frequency of binge drinking in the past month when compared to the 30 controls. It can be hypothesized that the increase in feedback information increased the students' desire to make changes in their behavior. While the purpose of Developing Readiness is not to change a person's behavior but to increase the willingness to engage in rehabilitation, these studies strongly suggest that personally relevant information and feedback can have motivational effects and thus increase a person's desire for change. Information may be particularly helpful to those in the contemplation stage of change to increase their desire to change, while feedback may most help those in the preparation stage to increase their sense of self-efficacy. The idea of motivational tailoring suggests that to successfully develop readiness for rehabilitation, it is important to understand how much someone wants to change, as well as how that individual wants or can use the help delivered, to do it.

Positive expectations for the future are less likely when a person does not understand what rehabilitation is or how it can help, because he may not believe the process to be supportive and thus be less likely to commit to change. On the other hand, people with higher levels of Commitment to Change are likely to feel more hopeful about the future and express more belief in the potential of rehabilitation and recovery to improve their futures. Littrell, Herth & Hinte (1996) found that "inner positive readiness and expectancy" was correlated with higher levels of hopefulness. Consumers have written about the importance of hope in rehabilitation and recovery (Lovejoy, 1982; Deegan, 1988; Leete, 1989). Deegan described the importance of hope and how the mental health system may extinguish hope in people who are living with psychiatric disability through low expectations and routine clinical practice. Researchers are beginning to demonstrate the importance of hope by correlating higher levels of hopefulness with rehabilitation outcomes. For example, Alverson, Alverson, Drake, and Becker (1998) showed that level of hopefulness was positively correlated with successful job search and retention. A study on recovery by Young and Ensing (1999) showed that for many participants, seeking out a source of hope and inspiration helps to foster the essential desire to change. In the words of one of these participants:

> It's inspiring, seeing other people, learning from people with mental illness... I learn from other people who say they've got a family to take care of, they have children to take care of, and they have meals to cook. I say wow, if they can do so much and I don't have nobody to be responsible for, at least I can try to get up and do something for myself" (Young & Ensing, p. 223).

Interviewing another consumer who has gone through the rehabilitation process can be a motivating activity that helps the person understand the benefits of that process in achieving a meaningful role. Participating in discussions of what psychiatric rehabilitation is or in "overview of psychiatric rehabilitation" sessions can reach consumers who tend to connect to others in a more intellectual manner than in an emotional manner. Motivational activities are selected based on the insights each client needs to develop to strengthen his motivation for change. Motivation is strengthened when the client participates in the activities selected and the meaning of these activities is explored with the client.

Increasing Commitment to Change involves increasing a person's belief in himself or herself—or self-efficacy—as well as increasing a belief in the potential of rehabilitation and recovery. People who have had few experiences of their strengths or who lack a belief in themselves are less committed to change. People who are more hopeful tend to have greater belief not only in the future but also in themselves. Several studies support the relation between expected outcomes, self-efficacy, and processes of change (Strecher, McEvoy, DeVellis, Becker & Rosenstock, 1986; Mudde, Kok & Strecher, 1995; Jinks, 1999; Prochaska, DiClemente, Velicer, Ginpil, & Norcross, 1985). Motivational Activities may increase hopefulness by influencing the expectations of the outcome of change (Ajzen & Fishbein, 1980; Rotter, 1982). Many motivational activities conducted during the process of Developing Readiness are activities that expose clients to the possibilities for positive outcomes, both in the achievement of the goal and the benefits of the rehabilitation process. Strong (1998) reports findings that suggest that practitioners can impact changes in self-concept, self-efficacy, and hopefulness by helping clients make connections with meaningful roles in organizations in the community. Practitioners and clients can plan activities that help clients feel more confident in their potential to gain or regain a role valued by the client. For example, a motivational activity like reading the consumer literature on recovery increases the client's awareness about the possibility of finding purpose and a meaningful role, despite the psychiatric disability. Participating in a series of meetings and exercises with other consumers who are all going through recovery in a recovery workshop (Spaniol, Koehler & Hutchinson, 1994) increases the person's hopefulness about the potential of recovery, provides practical information about techniques that have proven useful to others in their recovery, and provides accessible role models in the form of other consumers.

> **Increasing Commitment to Change involves increasing a person's belief in himself or herself— or self-efficacy— as well as increasing a belief in the potential of rehabilitation and recovery.**

Research also suggests several other strategies that can improve self-efficacy. Nelson (1998) describes a type of "solution focused" therapy using an intervention called "notice-the-difference." He proposes that identifying and duplicating small changes and improvements made by the client will empower the client to access his or her own resources to bring about necessary changes. This type of motivating activity is enhanced by using a journal to classify life changes through written communication (McClellan, Schneider & Perney, 1999), thus clarifying the personal implications of the activity.

Practitioners have helped their clients develop a range of experiences in which the client is certain to experience success as a way of building a stronger sense of self-efficacy. The practitioner can assist the client to integrate new knowledge gained in either a real experience or through a simulation. Such cognitive simulations help clients to begin to visualize themselves in a change process. Numerous research studies have found that these cognitive simulations enhance future performance (Bandura, 1986; Feltz & Landers, 1983; Kazdin, 1978) and strengthen a person's commitment to change (Bandura & Wood, 1989; Locke & Latham, 1990). This may be particularly effective for clients in the preparation stage. For example, one client who rated low on the Commitment to Change scale (Farkas et al., 2000) wanted and needed to develop more faith in his capacity as a student. He and his practitioner organized several educational experiences, over time, which ranged from a 2-hour class in calligraphy to a semester-long course at a community college in expository writing. After many of these small, success-based experiences, with support from his practitioner and others, his commitment to change increased, as did his self-awareness as a student, and his awareness of educational environments. He was then ready to begin to set an overall rehabilitation goal in an educational environment.

Awareness of the implications of new insights or the presence of a supportive person can increase a person's commitment to change. For example, another client managed to invite someone whom she had just met, to the movies for the first time. A supportive person was available to help her to reflect on what the experience might imply for the future. The facilitator helped her to see that if she could do something as difficult as inviting someone out to a movie for the first time, she might also be able to do other things that she had never done before.

Having a person who will support the client's participation in a rehabilitation process and is supportive of the kind of change the client is thinking of, will, also increase the client's commitment to change. In a study assessing the effects of support on depression in women recently diagnosed with cancer, Komproe, Rijken, Ros, and Winnubst (1997) show that available support has direct beneficial effects on depression, and received support has indirect effects, via improved appraisal of and coping with a stressful situation. Available support seems to increase people's positive feelings about the future and its possibilities. Connecting the person to a self-help group or a peer support network may enhance an individual's experience of being supported. Sometimes that sense of being supported stems from the presence of faith or a strong spiritual life rather than from some other person. Connecting consumers with spiritual groups, for those who are open to this method of connecting, can increase that person's commitment to change.

When Developing Readiness by helping a person to increase his or her commitment to change, practitioners will need to use hope-inspiring competencies as described by Russinova (1999) and Cohen, Nemec & Farkas, (2000). Russinova has identified these as ones that help the client to utilize interpersonal resources or ones that mobilize internal and external resources for recovery. A curriculum for the skills of "inspiring another" has been developed for use by practitioners and other facilitators (Cohen, Nemec & Farkas, 2000). Russinova (1999) makes the point that practitioners themselves need to examine the degree to which they feel hopeful about the potential their clients have to resume valued roles and recover from psychiatric disability. The skills to inspire can only be effective when used by a person who truly feels hopeful!

Developing Personal Closeness

A low rating on Personal Closeness can be due to a variety of factors. Sometimes, a low rating on Personal Closeness is the result of a mismatch between the client and practitioner. The client may have a style of connecting that is one the practitioner cannot provide. For example, a client may prefer to connect while engaged in some physical activity while the practitioner uses intellectual connection. Sometimes the only remedy for this situation is to have the client choose a different practitioner. A low rating on Personal Closeness can also be due to the client's lack of understanding of himself and the extent to which he feels he needs closeness with another. It may be due to his experience of the lack of positive support in the past. Engaging the client in relationships through activities that are meaningful to the client may increase the client's positive experience of personal closeness. For example, an individual may be isolated and unable to trust others in a relationship. The

> Sometimes, a low rating on Personal Closeness is the result of a mismatch between the client and practitioner.

most that person may be willing to accept is to have the practitioner sit with him, perhaps on a bench in a park and remain silent until the individual wishes to say something. The silence may last for weeks or even months. The practitioner's willingness to take the individual's lead and remain silent, for however long it takes, may provide the individual with his first experience of another person being willing to do the work needed to engage him. At times, helping a client work through structured exercises to increase his sense of connection to himself as well as to others, can help the person to experience relationships in a new way (Spaniol, Bellingham, Cohen & Spaniol, 2000).

Personal closeness to others is important in the overall recovery process, as well as being critical in rehabilitation. Young and Ensing (1999) recently demonstrated this finding. Collecting information from the client's perspective, they found that the pervasive effects of stigma and a fragile sense of self-worth make connecting with others and wanting to be close a particular challenge. Yet their study of recovery also revealed that, despite these difficulties, the role of interpersonal relationships between consumers was viewed as important in fostering the recovery process, including a readiness to engage in meaningful activities. Creating opportunities for positive interactions between consumers may, therefore, increase a person's openness to connecting with others, or their Personal Closeness ratings.

Developing Self-Awareness

A low rating on Self-Awareness can stem from a lack of experience or understanding of the self. Often people with serious psychiatric disabilities lack common life experiences that teach most people about their values and preferences in life. This lack of experience contributes to the disability and may be a great barrier in person's ability to set a goal (Martin et al., 1999). Many vocational counselors complain that their clients with psychiatric disabilities have unrealistic goals (Rogers et al., in press). Helping people experience real roles (e.g., internships, volunteer situations) can develop self-awareness with respect to their values and interests. These experiences need to be well-structured and short term because the goal of the experience is simply to give the person a basic understanding of some interests or values in order to increase the person's willingness to engage in rehabilitation. A longer experience might well require rehabilitation work to make it successful and would be more appropriately done during the rehabilitation process itself.

Two qualitative studies used a grounded theory approach in which an interview-based method of inquiry revealed some insights about how clients change. Jinks (1999) analyzed four clients' perceptions of change during long term counseling, and discovered that all felt more in control of their lives, as measured by increased self-awareness, confidence, insight, ability to make decisions and act to influence events, and assertiveness. Loysen (1996), in a study of 6 clients and their therapists, describes the change process in clients as a process of self-generativity, or "learning to be oneself in the world." This process is itself the result of three intertwined processes: building self-awareness, building self-acceptance, and separating self from others. Also emphasized is the genuineness of the client-therapist relationship, with the potential value of the therapist as a real person. A study in change by Scannell (1995), examined why men who are incarcerated

> Values clarification exercises or classes, interest tests, education about problem solving techniques or decision making styles are examples of educational or learning experiences that can be used to help individuals develop insight into their values, interests, and decision-making styles.

for violent crimes chose to request therapy. One of the primary reasons given was a heightened self-awareness and internal motivation that they needed to change. Targeted supportive psychotherapy, therefore, can be used as an activity to develop readiness for rehabilitation. Developing readiness activities are only designed to increase a person's understanding of themselves sufficiently that they are able to commit to a long process of change.

McFarlane and Lukens (1998) propose that education, training, and alterations of the social context foster insight, especially when those interventions include families, friends, other clients, and significant others. Values clarification exercises or classes, interest tests, education about problem solving techniques or decision making styles are examples of educational or learning experiences that can be used to help individuals develop insight into their values, interests, and decision-making styles—areas of insight that are relevant to increasing a person's willingness to begin the rehabilitation process. Portions of the "recovery workshop" include exercises that can help to increase a person's insight into their values and interests (Spaniol et al., 1994).

Young and Ensing (1999) identify gaining insight about the self as a middle phase of the process of recovery from severe psychiatric disability. Not only do people rediscover parts of the self that were temporarily lost, but they also discover and develop new potential and new self-growth as part of their internal exploration process. The rehabilitation process of choosing a goal helps clients to learn about their values and preferences. Knowing something about oneself, prior to beginning the process helps the client to engage and see value in what is to come.

Developing Environmental Awareness

A low rating on Environmental Awareness can be due to a lack of understanding about environments. Again people with psychiatric disabilities are often restricted in their opportunities to participate in a range of environments that is common to most people. Environmental awareness can be increased through experiences that expose people to a variety of settings they wish to explore. These experiences can be provided in a number of ways. Because the process of Developing Readi-

ness is not always linear and may instead parallel the approach/avoid
dynamic that is characteristic of the recovery process, it is important to
create multiple points of entry and levels of experience within programs
(Deegan, 1988). Rehabilitation programs can provide these experiences, especially if they provide environments that are flexible and
responsive to people at different stages of readiness. It is important to
offer people a wide variety of rehabilitation program options from
which to choose: supported work programs, transitional employment
programs, consumer run drop-in centers and businesses, workshops,
and skill training and supported education and to help individuals
understand what the different environments have to offer. This understanding can increase the person's willingness to engage in rehabilitation.

Environmental awareness can be increased in sequenced steps, tar-
geting an individual's current knowledge of environments. For example, if someone needs more information about work settings or experiences, she might participate in a series of activities to expose her to
work roles, settings, and opportunities. This new knowledge might be
sufficient to help the person internalize
the fact that if she engages in rehabilitation she may have access to a range of
different options as a goal, rather than
the same ones she had in the past in
which she did not succeed. During the
process of setting an overall rehabilitation goal itself, she will learn a lot more
about environmental options, perhaps,
by talking to peers and others who know
about work, doing some research into
various career options, and then by con-
ducting some informational interview-
ing or job shadowing. Informational interviewing and job shadowing
may also be useful in Developing Readiness, to help create a basic
understanding of the myriad of opportunities that might exist if a person chose to engage in a rehabilitation process. At the point of Developing Readiness, understanding that there are a variety of options is

> It is important to offer
people a wide variety of
rehabilitation program
options from which to choose:
supported work programs,
transitional employment
programs, consumer run
drop-in centers and
businesses, workshops, and
skill training and supported
education and to help
individuals understand what
the different environments
have to offer.

sufficient to helping increase the person's willingness to engage in rehabilitation.

A strategy that is particularly effective in increasing environmental awareness is facilitating persons with disabilities to serve as role models for one another. Young and Ensing's (1999) study on recovery showed that relationships formed with peer role models appeared to have a large impact on many of the participants. Additionally, a person need not be "fully recovered" to serve as a role model. Very often a person who is only few steps ahead of another person can be more effective than one whose achievements seem overly impressive (Deegan, 1988). These experiences are not only inspiring, but also they can provide concrete information about the kinds of settings and roles in which the role models exist, which will increase a client's awareness of environments. Seeing a consumer functioning as a professor in a university setting cannot only provide hope about possible outcomes but also introduce the idea of such an environment, its characteristics and demands more impactfully than many discussions about the same topic.

SUMMARY OF DEVELOPING READINESS

Table 7 summarizes the activities discussed in this section with respect to each readiness indicator. The activities identified in this section and summarized in Table 7 represent only some of the potential motivating activities that might be used to increase an individual's willingness to engage in rehabilitation.

Developing Readiness is a strategy to overcome barriers to being ready to set an overall rehabilitation goal. To overcome these barriers, the practitioner designs new experiences that will help the person develop a different perspective about their rehabilitation. By using the practitioner skills of increasing the client's exposure to motivating activities, clarifying any personal implications derived from the client's circumstances or exposure to these activities, and demonstrating credible support, the client's view of the change process of rehabilitation as desirable, possible and manageable is likely to be increased (Cohen, Forbess & Farkas, 2000). The practitioner's ability to use connecting

Table 7—Summary of Possible Developing Readiness Activities and Outcomes for Readiness Indicators

	Examples of Possible Activities	Outcomes of Activities
NEED *	Discussions, readings on recovery and rehabilitation research Speaking to other consumers Reviewing feedback on current performance Visiting; getting information about alternative environments	Increased dissatisfaction with current situation
COMMITMENT TO CHANGE	Recovery workshops Overviews of psychiatric rehabilitation Self-help groups Short term cognitive therapy "Walk and talk" activities to clarify personal implications	Increased desire for change
	Reading research Speaking to consumers who have been through the process Visiting psychiatric rehabilitation programs Recovery workshops	Increased positive expectations of change/hope
	Experience of positive role models "Notice the difference" interventions Cognitive simulations Small, success based experiences	Increased sense of self efficacy
	Identifying clients experience of those people available to support the client's wish for change/participation in rehabilitation Connecting with a self-help, peer group Connecting with a spiritual group	Increased sense of support

(continued)

Table 7—Summary of Possible Developing Readiness Activities and Outcomes for Readiness Indicators
(continued)

	Examples of Possible Activities	Outcomes of Activities
PERSONAL CLOSENESS	Changing practitioners to match client's style of connecting Accompanying activities Short, structured "connection" activities	Increased openness to forming connections with others
SELF-AWARENESS	Internships, short term volunteer work Targeted, supportive psychotherapy Recovery exercises and groups Education about values; interest tests	Increased understanding of values, interests, and decision making used in the past
ENVIRONMENTAL AWARENESS	Visits, informational interviewing, job shadowing across a variety of settings Access to a variety of rehabilitation program models Meeting with role models	Increased understanding that there are other settings and roles to strive for and that settings can vary by physical characteristics, type of people in them, and role demands

*Need can only be developed if the person has stated an interest in the idea of rehabilitation. Need can be further explored during the readiness assessment if the person perceives himself to be successful but the environment perceives him to be highly unsuccessful and in danger of losing his current environment.

skills (Cohen, Nemec & Farkas, 2000) throughout the process facilitates the client's openness to new experiences and insights.

What appears to make a difference to the development of readiness for rehabilitation is to have helpers who are motivated and prepared to reach out proactively to a wide range of clients, and offer interventions (motivational activities, clarification of personal implications, and demonstrations of credible support) that are matched to clients' stage of change (Cohen et al., 1997; Prochaska, 1999). Dr. Patricia Deegan, a clinical psychologist who is also a consumer-survivor, identified the elusiveness of the exact process of readiness, and the courage it takes to develop it. She talks about healing, a process that also requires a commitment to readiness. In "A Letter To My Friend Who Is Giving Up" (November 15, 1989), Deegan writes:

> "We can swing our legs over the side of the bed, stand up, face the promise and the pain of the day, seize the day and live it...This is the posture of recovery..."

> Healing does not happen quickly. We cannot will or command healing to happen. Healing happens at a level prior to what can be willed....We cannot will healing to happen to us. However...we can assume the posture of one who is surviving and recovering. We can swing our legs over the side of the bed, stand up, face the promise and the pain of the day, seize the day and live it...This is the posture of recovery... (p. 1).

Developing Readiness activities help individuals to see this "posture" as one that is desirable, possible, and manageable.

CHAPTER 5 *Conclusion*

Rehabilitation readiness reflects a person's willingness to engage in a specific process of change over at least 6 to 24 months. Facing the magnitude of the kinds of choices implied by the first component of psychiatric rehabilitation (i.e. setting an overall rehabilitation goal), or figuring out exactly what valued residential, vocational or educational role a person is willing to work for and in what setting they would prefer to perform that role, requires courage. That courage may be born out of a strong dissatisfaction with the current situation, a belief that change is desirable, likely to be positive and manageable, an openness to connecting with other people and a basic awareness of oneself and what environments might be like. The assessment of readiness involves evaluating these indicators to identify the extent to which a person with a serious psychiatric disability is more or less willing to try rehabilitation—at least at the point of the assessment. The assessment leads to a choice of strategies, one of which is to increase the person's readiness for rehabilitation. The development of readiness involves the encouragement of hopefulness and increased belief in the possibilities for the future.

> Readiness for rehabilitation requires some flicker of hope that recovery from impairment, disability and disadvantage is possible.

Readiness for rehabilitation requires some flicker of hope that recovery from impairment, disability and disadvantage is possible. Striving for a valued role —or rehabilitation— depends on this hope. Readiness for rehabilitation means a willingness to begin a journey, preferably with a supportive or helping person. The journey may involve acquiring new skills or resources that are not apparent in the moment. It may involve making the choice to continue the journey again and again over the course in time. Readiness for rehabilitation is a moment in time when the Self asks the implicit question: "Dare I even think about beginning to look at a dream for my future?" And answers: "I would like to try!"

References

Ajzen, I., & Fishbein, M. (1980). *Understanding and predicting social behavior.* Englewood, NJ: Prentice-Hall.

Alverson, H., Alverson, M., Drake, R. E., & Becker, D. R. (1998). Social correlates of competitive employment among people with severe mental illness. *Psychosocial Rehabilitation Journal, 22,* 34–40.

Amador, X. F. & David, A. S. (Eds.). (1998). *Insight and psychosis.* New York, NY: Oxford University Press.

Anderson, R. L. & Lewis, D. A. (1999). Clinical characteristics and service use of persons with mental illness living in an intermediate care facility. *Psychiatric Services, 50,* 1341–1345.

Annis, H. M., Schober, R., & Kelly, E. (1996). Matching addiction outpatient counseling to client readiness for change: The role of structured relapse prevention counseling. *Experimental and Clinical Psychopharmacology, 4,* 37–45.

Anthony, W. A. (1993). Recovery from mental illness: The guiding vision of the mental health service system in the 1990s. *Psychosocial Rehabilitation Journal, 16,* 11–23.

Anthony, W. A. (1994). Characteristics of people with psychiatric disabilities that are predictive of entry into the rehabilitation process and successful employment outcomes. *Psychosocial Rehabilitation Journal, 17*(3), 3–13.

Anthony, W. A., Cohen, M. R., & Farkas, M. D. (1987). Training and technical assistance in psychiatric rehabilitation. In A. T. Meyerson & T. Fine (Eds.), *Psychiatric disability: Clinical, legal, and administrative dimensions* (pp. 251–269). Washington, DC: American Psychiatric Press.

Anthony, W. A., Cohen, M. R., & Farkas, M. D. (1990). *Psychiatric rehabilitation.* Boston, MA: Boston University, Center for Psychiatric Rehabilitation.

Anthony, W. A., Cohen, M. R., Farkas, M. D., & Gagne, C. (2001). *Psychiatric rehabilitation* (2nd ed.). Boston, MA: Boston University, Center for Psychiatric Rehabilitation.

Anthony, W. A., Kennard, W. A., O'Brien, W., & Forbess, R. (1986). Psychiatric rehabilitation: Past myths and current realities. *Community Mental Health Journal, 22,* 249–264.

Bachelor, A. (1995). Clients' perception of the therapeutic alliance. *Journal of Counseling Psychology, 42,* 323–337.

Bandura, A. (1977). Self-efficacy: Toward a unifying theory of behavioral change. *Psychological Review, 84,* 191–215.

Bandura, A. (1986). The explanatory and predictive scope of self-efficacy theory. *Journal of Clinical and Social Psychology, 4,* 359–373.

Bandura, A. (1997). *Self-efficacy: The exercise of control.* New York: W.H. Freeman and Company.

Bandura, A., & Wood, R. E. (1989). Effect of perceived controllability and performance standards on self-regulation of complex decision-making. *Journal of Personality and Social Psychology, 56,* 5805–814.

Beels, C. (1981). Social support and schizophrenia. *Schizophrenia Bulletin,* 7(1), 58–72.

Bellack, A. S., & Mueser, K. T. (1990). Schizophrenia. In A. S. Bellack, M. Hersen, & A. E. Kazdin (Eds.), *International Handbook of Behavior Modification* (2nd ed., pp 353–369). New York: Plenum.

Blankertz, L., Robinson, S., Baron, T., Hughes, R., & Rutman, I. (1995). *A national survey of the psychosocial rehabilitation workforce. Report #1.* Matrix Research Institute, Philadelphia, PA.

Blume, A. W. & Schmaling, K. B. (1997). Specific classes of symptoms predict readiness to change scores among dually diagnosed patients. *Addictive Behaviors, 22,* 625–630.

Borsari, B. & Carey, K. B. (2000). Effects of a brief motivational intervention with college student drinkers. *Journal of Consulting and Clinical Psychology, 68,* 728–733.

Boston Center for Psychiatric Rehabilitation Consulting, Inc. (2001). *Psychiatric rehabilitation practitioner tools: Assessing and developing readiness.* Boston, MA: Boston University, Center for Psychiatric Rehabilitation.

Brenner, H., Hodel, B., Roder, V., & Corrigan, P. W. (1992). Treatment of cognitive dysfunction and behavior deficits in schizophrenia. *Schizophrenia Bulletin, 18,* 21–26.

Brown, V. B., Melchior, L. S., Panter, A. T., & Slaughter, R., & Huba, G. J. (2000). Women's steps of change and entry into drug abuse treatment: A multidimensional stages of change model. *Journal of Substance Treatment, 18,* 231–240.

Caras, S. (1994). Disabled: One more label. *Hospital and Community Psychiatry, 45,* 323–324.

Carkhuff, R. R. (1981). *Interpersonal skills and human productivity.* Amherst, MA: Human Resource Development Press.

Carkhuff, R. R. & Berenson, B. G. (1977). *Beyond counseling and therapy* (2nd ed.). NY: Holt, Rinehart & Winston.

Chamberlin, J. (1990). The ex-patients' movement: Where we've been and where we're going. *The Journal of Mind and Behavior, 11*(3-4), 323–336.

Chase, S. E. & Bell, C. S. (1990). Ideology, discourse, and gender: How gatekeepers talk about women school superintendents. *Social Problems, 37,* 163–177.

Ciompi, L. (1980). Catamnestic long-term study in the course of life and aging schizophrenics. *Schizophrenia Bulletin, 6,* 606–618.

Cohen, M. R., Anthony, W.A., & Farkas, M. D. (1997). Assessing and developing readiness for psychiatric rehabilitation. *Psychiatric Services, 8,* 644–646.

Cohen, M., Danley, K., & Nemec, P. (1985). *Psychiatric rehabilitation training technology: Direct skills teaching.* Boston, MA: Boston University, Center for Psychiatric Rehabilitation.

Cohen, M., Farkas, M., & Cohen, B. (1986). *Psychiatric rehabilitation training technology: Functional assessment.* Boston, MA: Boston University, Center for Psychiatric Rehabilitation.

Cohen, M., Farkas, M., Cohen, B., & Unger, K. (1991). *Psychiatric rehabilitation training technology: Setting an overall rehabilitation goal.* Boston, MA: Boston University, Center for Psychiatric Rehabilitation.

Cohen, M., Forbess, R. & Farkas, M. (2000). *Psychiatric rehabilitation training technology: Developing readiness for rehabilitation.* Boston, MA: Boston University, Center for Psychiatric Rehabilitation.

Cohen, M., Nemec, P., & Farkas, M. (2000). *Psychiatric rehabilitation training technology: Connecting for rehabilitation.* Boston, MA: Boston University, Center for Psychiatric Rehabilitation.

Cohen, M., Nemec, P., Farkas, M., & Forbess, R. (1988). *Psychiatric rehabilitation training technology: Case Management.* Boston, MA: Boston University, Center for Psychiatric Rehabilitation.

Colson D. (1986). Patient collaboration as a criterion for the therapeutic alliance. *Psychoanalytic Psychology, 5,* 259–268.

Corrigan, P. W., & Storzbach, D. (1993). The ecological validity of cognitive rehabilitation for schizophrenia. *The Journal of Cognitive Rehabilitation,* May, June.

Crites, J. (1961). A model for the measurement of vocational maturity. *Journal of Counseling Psychology, 8,* 255–259.

Curtis, L. C. (1993). Consumers as colleagues: Partnerships in the workforce. In Practice. Burlington, VT: Center for Community Change through Housing and Support, Institute for Program Development, Trinity College of Vermont.

Danley, K. S. (1997). *The choose-get-keep approach to employment support: An intervention manual.* Boston, MA: Boston University, Center for Psychiatric Rehabilitation.

Danley, K. S., Sciarappa, K., & MacDonald-Wilson, K. (1992). Choose-get-keep: A psychiatric approach to supported employment. *New Directions in Mental Heath Services, 53,* 87–96.

Davidson, L.D. & Strauss, J.S. (1992). Sense of self in recovery from severe mental illness. *British Journal of Psychiatry, 65,* (1), 131–145.

Deegan, P. E. (1988). Recovery: The lived experience of rehabilitation. *Psychosocial Rehabilitation Journal, 11,* 11–19.

Deegan, P. (1989). *A letter to my friend who is giving up.* Keynote Address, Connecticut Conference on Supported Employment, Treadway Cromwell Hotel, Cromwell, CT. November 15, 1989.

Deegan, P. E. (1997). Recovery and empowerment for people with psychiatric disabilities. *Social Work in Health Care, 25*(3), 11–24.

DeHoff, S. L. (1998). In search of a paradigm for psychological and spiritual growth: Implications for psychotherapy and spiritual direction. *Pastoral Psychology, 46,* 333–346.

Drake, R. E., Becker, D. R, Biesanz, J. C., Torrey, W. C., McHugo, G. J., & Wyzik, P. F. (1994). Rehabilitation day treatment vs. supported employment: I. Vocational outcomes. *Community Mental Health Journal, 30,* 519–532.

Drake, R. E., Becker, D. R., Beisanz, J. C., & Wyzik, P. F. (1996). Day treatment vs. supported employment for people with severe mental illness: A replication study. *Psychiatric Services, 17*(10), 1125–1127.

Egan, G. (1994). *The skilled helper: A problem-management approach to helping* (5th Edition). Pacific Grove, CA: Brooks/Cole.

Farkas, M., Anthony, W. A. & Cohen, M. R. (1989). An overview of psychiatric rehabilitation: The approach and its programs. In M. Farkas & W. A. Anthony (Eds.), *Psychiatric rehabilitation programs: Putting theory into practice.* Baltimore, MD: Johns Hopkins University Press, 1–27.

Farkas, M., Cohen, M., McNamara, S., Nemec, P., & Cohen, B. (2000). *Psychiatric rehabilitation training technology: Assessing readiness for rehabilitation.* Boston, MA: Boston University, Center for Psychiatric Rehabilitation.

Farkas, M., Gagne, C. & Anthony, W. A. (1997). *Rehabilitation and recovery: A paradigm for the new millennium.* Monograph, Center for Psychiatric Rehabilitation, Boston University, Boston, MA.

Felton, C. J., Stastny, P., Shern, D. L., Blanch, A., Donahue, Knight, & Brown. (1995). Consumers as peer specialists on intensive case management teams: Impact on client outcomes. *Psychiatric Services, 46,* 1037–1044.

Feltz, D. L. & Landers, D. M. (1983). Effects of mental practice on motor skill learning and performance: A meta-analysis. *Journal of Sports Psychology, 5,* 25–57.

Ferrari, M. D. & Sternberg, R. J. (Eds.) (1998). *Self-awareness: Its nature and development.* New York, NY: The Guilford Press.

Fisher, D. (1994). New vision of healing: A reasonable accommodation for consumer/survivors working as mental health services providers. *Psychosocial Rehabilitation Journal, 17,* 67–82.

Frieswyk, S., Colson, D. B., Coyne, L., Gabbard, G., Horwitz, L. & Newsom, G. (1986). Therapeutic alliance: Place as process and outcome variable in dynamic psychotherapy research. *Journal of Consulting and Clinical Psychology, 54,* 32–39.

Gaitz, L.M. (1984). Chronic mental illness in aged patients. In M. Mirabi (Ed.), *The chronically mentally ill: Research and services,* (pp. 281–290). Jamaica, NY: Spectrum Publications.

Geczy, B., Jr. & Sultenfuss, J. (1995). Group psychotherapy on state hospital admission wards. *International Journal of Group Psychotherapy, 45,* 1–15.

Gehrs, M. & Goering, P. (1994). The relationship between the working alliance and rehabilitation outcomes of schizophrenia. *Psychosocial Rehabilitation Journal, 18*(2), 43–54.

Gold, N. (1990). Motivation: The crucial but unexplored component of social work practice. *Social Work, 35,* 49–56.

Goldman, H. H., Gattozzi, A. A., & Taube, C.A. (1981). Defining and counting the chronically mentally ill. *Hospital and Community Psychiatry, 32,* 21–27.

Granger, D. (1994). *Recovery from mental illness: A first person perspective of an emerging paradigm.* Paper presented at the National Forum on Recovery for Persons with Severe Mental Illness, Columbus, OH.

Harding, C. M., Brooks, G.W., Ashikaga, T., Strauss, J. S. & Breier, A. (1987a). The Vermont longitudinal study of persons with severe mental illness: I. Methodology, study sample, and overall status 32 years later. *American Journal of Psychiatry, 144,* 718–726.

Harding, C. M., Brooks, G. W., Ashikaga, T. Strauss, J. S. & Breier, A. (1987b). The Vermont longitudinal study: II. Long-term outcome of subjects who retrospectively met DSM-III criteria for schizophrenia. *American Journal of Psychiatry, 144,* 727–735.

Harding, C. & Zahniser, J. (1994). Empirical correction of seven myths about schizophrenia with implications for treatment. *Acta Psychiatrica Scandinavica Supplementum, 90* (Suppl 384), 140–146.

Harding C., Zubin, J., & Strauss, J. (1992). Chronicity in schizophrenia: Revisited. *British Journal of Psychiatry, 161,* 27–37.

Harris, M. & Bergman, H. C. (1987). Differential treatment planning for young adult chronic patients. *Hospital and Community Psychiatry, 38,* 638–643.

Hill, S. W. (1997). Readiness for rehabilitation. *Psychiatric Services, 48,* 1594.

Hiroto, D. S. & Seligman, M. E. (1975). Generality of learned helplessness in man. *Journal of Personality and Social Psychology, 31,* 311–327.

Holland, J. (1985). *Making vocational choices: A theory of vocational personalities and work environments.* (2nd ed.). Englewood Cliffs, NJ: Prentice Hall.

Houghton, J. F. (1982). First person account: Maintaining mental health in a turbulent world. *Schizophrenia Bulletin, 8,* 548–552.

International Association of Psychosocial Rehabilitation Services. (1997). New prevalence estimates of serious mental illness. *IAPSRS Newsletter, 8*(10). Columbia, MD.

Janis, I. L. & Mann, L. (1977). *Decision making: A psychological analysis of conflict, choice, commitment.* Free Press: New York.

Jinks, G. H. (1999). Intentionality and awareness: A qualitative study of clients' perceptions of change during longer term counseling. *Counseling Psychology Quarterly, 12,* 57–71.

Kalman, T. P. (1983). An overview of patient satisfaction with psychiatric treatment. *Hospital and Community Psychiatry, 34,* 48–54.

Kazdin, A. E. (1978). Covert modeling: The therapeutic application of imagined rehearsal. In J. L. Singer & K. S. Pope (Eds.), *The power of human imagination: New methods in psychotherapy.* (pp. 255–278). New York: Plenum.

Kelly, C. M, Keany, H., &. Glueckauf, R. L. (1993). Disability and value change: An overview and reanalysis of acceptance of loss theory. *Rehabilitation Psychology, 38.*

Kelly, M. E., van Kammen, D. P., & Allen, D. N. (1999). Empirical validation of primary negative symptoms: Independence from effects of medication and psychosis. *American Journal of Psychiatry, 156*(3), 406–411.

Kern, R. S. & Green, M. F. (1998). Cognitive remediation in schizophrenia. In K.T. Mueser and N. Tarrier et al., (Eds.), *Handbook of social functioning in schizophrenia.* (pp. 342–354). Boston, MA: Allyn & Bacon, Inc.

Komproe, I. H., Rijken, M., Ros, W. J. K., Winnubst, J. A. M., & Hart, H. (1997). Available support and received support: Different effects under stressful circumstances. *Journal of Social and Personal Relationships, 14,* 59–77.

Kramer, P., Anthony, W., Rogers, E. S., & Kennard, W. (1999). *Integrating psychiatric rehabilitation technology into assertive community treatment.* Unpublished manuscript. Boston, MA: Boston University, Center for Psychiatric Rehabilitation.

Kramer, P. J. & Gagne, C. G. (1997). Barriers in recovery and empowerment for people with psychiatric disabilities. In L. Spaniol, C. Gagne, & M. Koehler (Eds.), *Psychological and social aspects of psychiatric disability,* (pp. 467–476). Boston, MA: Boston University, Center for Psychiatric Rehabilitation.

Lee, P., Lieh-Mak, F., & Spinks, J. (1993). Coping strategies of people with schizophrenia. *British Journal of Psychology, 163,* 177–182.

Leete, E., (1989). How I perceive and manage my illness. *Schizophrenia Bulletin, 8*(4), 197–200.

Littrell, K. H., Herth, K. A., & Hinte, L. E. (1996). The experience of hope in adults with schizophrenia. *Psychiatric Rehabilitation Journal, 19*(4), 61–65.

Locke, E. A. & Latham, G. P. (1990). *The theory of goal setting and task performance.* Englewood Cliffs, NJ: Prentice-Hall.

Lovejoy, M. (1982). Expectations and recovery process. *Schizophrenia Bulletin, 8*(4), 605–609.

Loysen ,T. (1996). Developing a sense of self in psychotherapy. *Dissertation Abstracts International: Section B: The Sciences and Engineering, 57* (2-B): 1447.

Marcus, B. H., Emmons, K. M., Simkin-Silverman, L. R., Linnan, L. A., Taylor, E. R., Bock, B. C., Roberts, M. B., Rossi, J. S., & Abrams, D. B. (1998). Evaluation of motivationally tailored vs. standard self-help physical activity interventions at the workplace. *American Journal of Health Promotion, 12,* 246–253.

Markus, H., & Nurius, P. (1986). Possible selves. *American Psychologist, 41,* 954–969.

Martin, R., Rogers, E. S., & Farkas, M. (1999). *Assessing change in clients in a vocational rehabilitation program.* Boston University, Center for Psychiatric Rehabilitation. Manuscript in preparation.

McClellan, M. L., Schneider, M. F., & Perney, J. (1999). Rating (life task action) change in journal excerpts and narratives using Prochaska, DiClemente, and Norcross's Five Stages of Change. *Journal of Individual Psychology, 54,* 546–559.

McConnaughy, E. A., DiClemente, C. C., Prochaska, J. O., & Velicer, W. F. (1989). Stages of change in psychotherapy: A follow-up report. *Psychotherapy, 26*(4), 494–503.

McConnaughy, E. A., Prochaska, J. O., & Velicer, W. F. (1983) Stages of change in psychotherapy: Measurement and sample profiles. *Psychotherapy, 26,* 494–503.

McCrory, D. J., Connolly, P. S., Hanson-Mayer, T. P., Sheridan-Landolfi, J. S., Barone, F. C., Blood, A. H., & Gilson, A. M. (1980). The rehabilitation crisis: The impact of growth. *Journal of Applied Rehabilitation Counseling, 11,* 136–139.

McDermott, B. (1990). Development of an instrument for assessing self-efficacy in schizophrenic spectrum disorders. *Journal of Clinical Psychology, 51*(3), 320–331.

McFarlane, W. R & Lukens, E. P. (1998). Insight, families, and education: An exploration of the role of attribution in clinical outcome. In X. F. Amador and A.S. David et al. (Eds.), *Insight and Psychosis* (pp. 317–331). New York, NY: Oxford University Press.

Moxley, D. P. (1994). Serious mental illness and the concept of recovery: Implications for social work practice in psychiatric rehabilitation. *Psychiatric Rehabilitation and Community Support Monograph 1*(5). Boston University, Center for Psychiatric Rehabilitation, Boston, MA.

Moxley, D. P. & Mowbray, C. T. (1997). Consumers as providers: Forces and factors legitimizing role innovation in psychiatric rehabilitation In C. T. Mowbray, D. P. Moxley, C. A. Jasper & L. L. Howell (Eds.), *Consumers as providers in psychiatric rehabilitation,* (pp. 2–35). Columbia, MD: IAPSRS.

Mudde, A. N., Kok, G., & Strecher. V. J. (1995). Self-efficacy as a predictor for the cessation of smoking: Implications for smoking cessation program. *Psychological Health, 10,* 353–67.

Musser-Granski, J. & Carrillo, D. F. (1997). The use of bilingual, bicultural paraprofessionals in mental health services: Issues for hiring, training and supervision. *Community Mental Health Journal, 33*(1), 51–60.

National Institute of Mental Health. (1987). *Toward a model plan for a comprehensive, community based mental health system.* Rockville, MD: Division of Education and Service Systems Liaison.

Nelson, V. (1998). Notice the difference. *Journal of Family Psychotherapy, 9,* 81–84.

Norcross, J. C. & Prochaska, J. O. (1986). Psychotherapist heal thyself: I. The psychological distress and self-change of psychologists, counselors, and laypersons. *Psychotherapy, 23,* 102–114.

Nunn, K. P. (1996). Personal hopefulness: A conceptual review of the relevance of the perceived future to psychiatry. *British Journal of Medical Psychology, 69* (3), 3–20.

Ogawa, K., Miya, M., Watari, A., Nakazawa, M., Yuasa, S., & Utena, H. (1987). A long-term follow-up study of schizophrenia in Japan with special reference to the course of social adjustment. *British Journal of Psychiatry, 151,* 758–765.

Pelletier, J. R., Rogers, E. S. & Thruer, S. (1985). The mental health needs of individuals with severe psychiatric disability: A consumer advocate perspective. *Rehabilitation Literature, 46,* 186–193.

Pepper, B. & Ryglewicz, H. (Eds). (1984). Advances in treating the young adult chronic patient *(New Directions for Mental Health Services, No. 21).* San Francisco:Jossey-Bass.

Prochaska, J. O. (1991). Prescribing to the stage and level of change. *Psychotherapy, 28,* 463–468.

Prochaska, J. O. (1996). A stage paradigm for integrating clinical and public health approaches to smoking cessation. *Addictive Behaviors, 21,* 721–732.

Prochaska, J. O. (1999). How do people change and how can we change to help many more people? In M.A. Hubble and B.L. Duncan et al. (Eds.), *The heart and soul of change: What works in therapy* (pp. 227–255). Washington, DC: American Psychological Association.

Prochaska, J. O. & DiClemente, C. C. (1984). *The transtheoretical approach: Crossing traditional boundaries of therapy.* Homewood, IL: Dow Jones-Irwin.

Prochaska, J. O., DiClemente, C. C., & Norcross, J. C. (1992). In search of how people change: Applications to addictive behaviors. *American Psychologist, 47,* 1102–1114.

Prochaska, J. O., DiClemente, J. M., Velicer, W. F., Ginpil, S., & Norcross, J. (1985). Predicting change in smoking status for self-changers. *Addictive Behaviors, 10,* 395–406.

Prochaska, J. O. & Prochaska, J. M. (1999). Why don't continents move? Why don't people change? *Journal of Psychotherapy Integration, 9,* 83–102.

Prochaska, J. O., Velicer, W. F., DiClemente, C. C. & Fava, J. (1988). Measuring processes of change: Applications to the cessation of smoking. *Journal of Consulting and Clinical Psychology, 56,* 520–528.

Reiss, S. (1987). Symposium overview: Mental health and mental retardation. *Mental Retardation, 25,* 323–324.

Relich, J. D., Debus, R. L., & Walker, R. (1986). The mediating role of attribution and self-efficacy variables for treatment effects on achievement outcomes. *Contemporary Educational Psychology, 11,* 195–216.

Rogers, C. R. (1957). The necessary and sufficient conditions of therapeutic personality change. *Journal of Consulting Psychology, 21,* 95–103.

Rogers, C. R. (1961). *On becoming a person.* Boston, MA: Houghton Mifflin Company.

Rogers, E. S., Cohen, B. F., Danley, K. S., Hutchinson, D. & Anthony, W. (1986). Training mental health workers in psychiatric rehabilitation. *Schizophrenia Bulletin, 12,* 709–719.

Rogers, E. S., Danley, K. S., Anthony, W. A., Martin, R., & Walsh, D. (1994). The residential needs and preferences of persons with serious mental illness: A comparison of consumers and family members. *The Journal of Mental Health Administration, 21*(1), 42–51.

Rogers, E. S., Martin, R., Anthony, W., Massaro, J., Danley, K., & Crean, T. (In press). Assessing readiness for change among persons with severe mental illness. *Community Mental Health Journal.*

Rotter, J. B. (1982). Social learning theory. In N.T. Feather (Ed.), *Expectations and actions: Expectancy-value models in psychology* (pp. 241–260). Hillsdale, NJ: Erlbaum.

Ruggeri, M., Leese, M.,Thorncroft, G., & Tansella, M. (2000). Definition and prevalence of severe and persistent mental illness. *British Journal of Psychiatry, 177,* 149–155.

Russinova, Z. (1999, Oct/Nov/Dec). Providers' hope-inspiring competence as a factor optimizing psychiatric rehabilitation outcomes. *Journal of Rehabilitation,* 50–57.

Russinova, Z., Ellison, M. & Foster, R. (1999). *Survey of professionals and managers with psychiatric disabilities.* Presentation at IAPSRS, 24th Annual conference, Minneapolis, MN, May 10–14.

Salit, S. A., Kuhn, E. M., Hartz, A. J., Vu, J. M. & Mosso, A. L. (1998). Hospitalization costs associated with homelessness in New York City. *The New England Journal of Medicine, 338*(24), 1734–1763.

ᴐ.

ɔ7

ⁿt offenders in jail: Why they choose to enter ther-
⸗ *International: Section B: The Sciences and*
ɔ462.

ᵤn, T. P. (1985). Modeled importance of task strategies
ᵤt beliefs: Effect on self-efficacy and skill development.
⸗arly Adolescence, 5, 247–258.

⸗., Balch, P., & Flynn, T. C. (1984). Assessing a CMHC's impact:
⸗ᵤdent and gatekeeper awareness of center services. *Journal of Communi-*
.y Psychology, 12, 61–66.

Segal, S., Silverman, C., & Baumohl, J. (1989). Seeking person-environment fit in community care placement. *Journal of Social Issues, 45*(3), 49–64.

Shern, D. L., Felton, C. J., Hough, R. L., Lehman, A. F., Goldfinger, S., Valencia, E., Dennis, D., Straw, R., & Wood, P. A. (1997). Housing outcomes for homeless adults with mental illness: Results from the Second Round McKinney Program. *Psychiatric Services, 48,* 239–241.

Shern, D. L., Tsemberis, S., Anthony, W. A., Lovell, A.M., Richmond, L., Felton, V.J., Winarski, J. & Cohen, M. (2000). Serving street dwelling individuals with psychiatric disabilities: Outcomes of a psychiatric rehabilitation clinical trial. *American Journal of Public Health, 90,* 1873–1878.

Shern, D. L., Tsemberis, S. Winarski, J., Cope, N., Cohen, M. R., & Anthony,W.A. (1997). The effectiveness of psychiatric rehabilitation for persons who are street dwelling with serious disability related to mental illness. In W.R. Breakey and J.W. Thompson (Eds), *Mentally ill and homeless: Special programs for special needs.* Amsterdam, Netherlands: Harwood Academic.

Silverstein, S. M., Hitzel, H., & Schenkel. L. (1998). Identifying and addressing cognitive barriers to rehabilitation readiness. *Psychiatric Services, 49,* 43–46.

Snow, M. G., Prochaska, J. O., & Rossi, J. S. (1992). Processes of change in alcoholic anonymous: Maintenance factors in long-term sobriety. *Journal of Studies on Alcohol,* 362–371.

Solomon, P., Draine, J., & Delaney, M. A. (1995). The working alliance and consumer case management. *The Journal of Mental Health Administration, 22,* 126–134.

Spaniol, L., Bellingham, R., Cohen, B.F., & Spaniol, S. (2000) *Connectedness : Some skills for personal growth.* Boston, MA: Boston University, Center for Psychiatric Rehabilitation. Manuscript in preparation.

Spaniol, L., Gagne, C., & Koehler, M. (1999). Recovery from serious mental illness: What it is and how to support people in their recovery. In R. P. Marinelli & A. E. Dell Orto (Eds.), *The psychological and social impact of disability* (4th ed.). New York: Springer Publishing.

Spaniol, L., Koehler, M., & Hutchinson, D. (1994). *Recovery workbook: Practical coping and empowerment strategies for people with psychiatric disability.* Boston, MA: Boston University, Center for Psychiatric Rehabilitation.

Strauss, J. S. (1986). Discussion: What does rehabilitation accomplish? *Schizophrenia Bulletin, 12,* 720–723.

Strauss, J. S., Hafez, H., Lieberman, P., & Harding, C. M. (1985). The course of psychiatric disorder, III: Longitudinal principles. *American Journal of Psychiatry, 142,* (3), 289–296.

Strecher, V. J., McEvoy, M., DeVellis, B. M., Becker, M. H., & Rosenstock, I. M. (1986). The role of self-efficacy in achieving health behavior change. *Health Education Quarterly, 13,* 73–91.

Strong, S. (1998). Meaningful work in supportive environments: Experiences with the recovery process. *American Journal of Occupational Therapy, 52,* 31–38

Struening, E. L. & Padgett, D. K. (1990). Physical health status, substance use and abuse, and mental disorders among homeless adults. *Journal of Social Issues, 46*(4), 65–81.

Stuve, P., Erickson, R.C., & Spaulding, W. (1991). Cognitive rehabilitation: The next step in psychiatric rehabilitation. *Psychosocial Rehabilitation Journal, 15,* 9–26.

Substance Abuse and Mental Health Services Administration. (1993). *SAMSHA strategic plan.* Washington, DC: US Department of Health and Human Services.

Sullivan, A. P., Nicolellis, D., Danley, K. S., & MacDonald-Wilson, K. (1993). Choose-get-keep: A psychiatric rehabilitation approach to supported education. *Psychosocial Rehabilitation Journal, 17*(1), 55–68.

Tanzman B. (1993). An overview of surveys of mental health consumers' preferences for housing and support services. *Hospital and Community Psychiatry, 44,* 450–455.

Tayler, D., Piagesi, D., McNaught, J., & Nielson, M. (1989). A psychiatric rehabilitation approach in a clubhouse setting: Sussex House, Newton, NJ. In M. Farkas and W. A. Anthony (Eds.), *Psychiatric rehabilitation: Putting Theory into practice.* Baltimore, MD: Johns Hopkins University Press.

Thompson, J., Flynn, R., & Griffith, S. (1994). Congruence and coherence as predictions of congruent employment outcomes. *Career Development Quarterly, 42,* 271–281.

Tsang, H., Lam, P., Ng, B. & Leung, O. (2000). Predictors of employment outcome for people with psychiatric disabilities: A review of the literature since the mid-1980s. *Journal of Rehabilitation, 66*(2), 19–35.

Tsuang, M. T., & Winokur, G. (1975). The Iowa 500: field work in a 35-year follow-up of depression, mania, and schizophrenia. *Canadian Psychiatric Association Journal, 20,* 359–365.

⌐., & Fleming, J. A. (1979). Long-term outcome of ⌐phrenia and affective disorders compared with ⌐m-free surgical conditions. *Archives of General Psy-* ⌐301.

⌐er, M. Teague, G. B., Fallot, R. D. (1999). Effective treatment ⌐ps for persons with serious psychiatric disorders: The importance ⌐nment states of mind. *Journal of Counseling and Clinical Psycholo-* ⌐7(5), 725–732.

⌐icer, W. F., Rossi, J. S., DiClemente, C. C., & Prochaska, J. O. (1996). A criterion measurement model for health behavior change. *Addictive Behaviors, 21,* 555–584.

Walker, K. S. (1999). Analysis of client readiness for change: Variation by type and intensity of motivational distress (readiness for change). *Dissertation Abstracts International: Section A: Humanities and Social Sciences, 60* (5-A); 1465.

Wallston, B. S., Hoover-Dempsey, K. B., Brissie, J. S., & Rozee-Koker, P. (1989). Gatekeeping transactions: Women's resource acquisition and mental health in the workplace. *Psychology of Women Quarterly, 13,* 205–222.

Ware, N. C. & Goldfinger, S. M. (1997). Poverty and rehabilitation in severe psychiatric disorders. *Psychiatric Rehabilitation Journal, 21*(1), 3–9.

Wasylenki, D., Goering, P., Lancee, W., Ballantyne, R., & Farkas, M. (1985). Impact of a case manager program on psychiatric aftercare. *Journal of Nervous and Mental Disease, 173,* 303–308.

Weiner, B. (1985). An attributional theory of achievement motivation and emotion. *Psychological Review, 92,* 548–573.

Wood, P. H. (1980). Appreciating the consequences of disease: The classification of impairments, disability, and handicaps. *The WHO Chronicle, 34,* 376–380.

Young, S. L. & Ensing, D. S. (1999). Exploring recovery from the perspective of people with psychiatric disabilities. *Psychosocial Rehabilitation Journal, 22,* 219–231.

Zimmerman, G.L., Olsen, C.G., & Boworth, M.F. (2000). A 'stages of change' approach to helping patients change behavior. *American Family Physician, 61,* 1409–1416.

Zipple, A., Drouin, M., Armstrong, M., Brooks, M., Flynn, J., & Buckley, W. (1997). Consumers as colleagues: Moving beyond ADA compliance. In C. T. Mowbray, D. P. Moxley, C.A. Jasper & L.L. Howell (Eds.), *Consumers as providers in psychiatric rehabilitation* (406–418). Columbia, MD: Colbourn House Publishing and Marketing.